The Breath of God

OTHER BOOKS BY NANCY ROTH

We Sing of God: A Hymnal for Children
Praying: A Book for Children
A Closer Walk: Meditating on Hymns for Year A
Awake My Soul! Meditating on Hymns for Year B
New Every Morning: Meditations on Hymns for Year C
Praise My Soul: Meditating on Hymns
Meditations for Choir Members
Organic Prayer
An Invitation to Christian Yoga (book and CD)
Spiritual Exercises

THE BREATH
of GOD

Nancy Roth

SEABURY BOOKS
an imprint of Church Publishing, Inc., New York

Published in the United States of America by Church Publishing,
Inc. No portion of this book may be reproduced, stored in or
introduced into a retrieval system, or transmitted, in any form
or by any means—including photocopying—without the prior
written permission of Church Publishing, except in the case of
brief quotations embedded in critical articles and reviews.

Library of Congress Cataloging-in-Publication Data

Roth, Nancy, 1936–
  Breath of God / Nancy Roth.
      p.   cm.
  Originally published: Cambridge, Mass. : Cowley Publications,
c1990.
  Includes bibliographical references and index.
  ISBN-13: 978-1-59627-032-9 (alk. paper)
  ISBN-10: 1-59627-032-2 (alk. paper)
  1. Prayer. I. Title.
  BV215.R67 2006
  248.3'2--dc22

                                    2006017017

Church Publishing, Inc.
445 Fifth Avenue
New York, New York 10016
www.churchpublishing.org

To Bob,
with whom I have shared life and breath
for the better part
(in every sense of the word)
of life's journey

Contents

Acknowledgments

I wish to acknowledge my debt to my many teachers of prayer, both those who have taught me in person and those who have taught me through their books, in particular Evelyn Underhill, Friedrich von Hügel, Thomas Merton, and Douglas Steere. I am happy to have discovered Donna Farhi's *The Breathing Book* recently; her insights have contributed immeasurably to the exercises in this edition.

I wish also to thank my editor and friend Cynthia Shattuck, with whom, as always, it has been a pleasure to work.

Finally, I count myself blessed to have married, over forty years ago, a husband whose patience, good advice, and support make it possible to fit the writing of books into an already busy life.

Foreword

My own experience of reading *The Breath of God* was both refreshing and arresting. Quietly absorbing each evocative image, I found myself drawn into an experience of prayer and invited to allow the Holy Breath to freshen and reshape my thoughts and attitudes about prayer.

The central metaphor, breath, God's and ours, as Nancy Roth unfolds and develops it, situates our experience of God in prayer in our most basic life process. Breath is life. God's Spirit in every religious tradition is described as source of the life breath and intimately associated with air and wind as well. Because the human process of respiration is dependent on the entire ecosystem that supports it, the metaphor of breathing is intrinsically relational, interactive, and constant.

Although breathing is a continuous process, it often escapes our conscious attention even while it sustains us in all other activities. How like our relationship to God! We are continually nourished by the Holy Breath whether or not we deliberately respond. In this context, God is discovered to be already present in our lives. We need only to become present to ourselves in the most ordinary of ways to find that God is breathing us into life and love. And we can joyously savor and respond to that amazing reality.

Every section of this book reveals God to be wholly available in the ordinary round that comprises our days. Nancy is a sure teacher of prayer. She draws on her extensive experience helping others to pray and allows us to experience her praying in her daily round of family life, teaching, preaching, dancing, and creating. Her practical suggestions and credible examples help us believe that we need no special circumstances to enter the domain of prayer, and that it is relatively simple to enter it for the first time or to reenter it again at any time.

The view of growth in the life of prayer presented in these pages is radically nonlinear. "In geometric terms it is an expanding circle rather than an ascending line," Nancy notes. "The metaphor of breath suggests that 'progress' in the life of prayer is more like the expansion of the capacity of the lungs than movement along a single path toward a goal." It would appear this increased capacity is more a criterion of progress than any of the more common "ascents." This nonlinear feel for the life of prayer animates her description of various forms of prayer so that none is "better" than any other, yet each has its honored place in our prayer life, dependent on circumstances and attraction.

The gracefulness and force of Nancy's poetically evocative language delights, refreshes, and illumines. In itself it creates the "holy spaciousness" needed to sustain a life of prayer. One might well argue that we encounter here an embodied and metaphorical theology. This treatment of prayer is reverently inclusive of all aspects of the human: embodiment, action, interiority, rationality, intuition, and artistic creativity.

As earthlings, we belong to the earth. Poetic reflections rooted in experiences of the physical universe expand our sense of wonder at the intricacy and variety of the physical world and ground us in relationship to this creator-God who breathes life into us. Nancy's artistic perceptions likewise demonstrate the intimate relationship between aesthetic experiences and prayer. Experiences with dance, music, and the visual arts enliven the text and expand our perceptions through engagement with non-linguistic forms of knowing.

Finally, Nancy's perspective is broadly ecumenical. She draws examples and cites authors from diverse spiritual traditions. Quakers, Eastern Orthodox writers, and saints and mystics from the common Christian tradition are equally at home in these pages. This simple and evocative invitation to begin to pray, or to return to prayer, will be widely received by many who share this very basic desire to be more fully alive in God.

—JANET RUFFING,
FORDHAM UNIVERSITY

God's Breath

Notice your breath as you begin reading this book. Is it calm and steady? Or is it slowing down gradually, as you relax after hurrying through some tasks in order to have time for reading?

Now think about your breath at various times in your life. Do you remember how your breathing felt when you were anxious, perhaps because you were uncomfortable about speaking in public or concerned that you would be late for an important appointment? When you finally found everything to be all right, did you relax with a deep sigh? Do you remember the steady calm of your breathing at those moments when you have been most at peace? Do you remember gasping when startled? Have you ever felt short of breath? Or have you ever hyperventilated, feeling light-headed because your lungs contained an imbalance of oxygen and carbon dioxide?

As you think about these moments in your life, you probably realize that your oxygen requirement can be a fairly accurate barometer of your emotional or "spiritual" state. The English word "spiritual" finds its root in the Latin *spiritus*, which means both "breath" and "spirit." Equivalent words in Hebrew and in Greek are *ruach* and *pneuma*. Both breath and spirit bring us to life, or "inspire" us. And there, in all its simplicity and depth, we find the connection between prayer and the life-giving breath of God. Just as breath constantly renews the body, filling the lungs with oxygen and emptying the lungs of carbon dioxide, so also our prayer constantly opens us to God's life within us and helps us empty ourselves of those things that are alien to fullness of life.

The Christian spiritual tradition provides us with many metaphors that illustrate the process of growth in the life of prayer. Often these metaphors suggest that we move from one way of praying to other "more advanced" ways as we grow and mature. They are images of ladders, of mountains, of journeys: metaphors conveying linear movement.

Ladders, mountains, and journeys tell only one side of the story, however. In this book, I use the image of the breath—a basic human function—both as a metaphor for prayer and as a means of understanding the integration of prayer and daily life. In geometric terms, it is an expanding circle rather than an ascending line. The metaphor of breath suggests that "progress" in the life of prayer is more like the expansion of the capacity of the lungs than movement along a single path toward a goal.

I have brought to this book my personal history as well as my professional training. My history includes both the self-conscious breathlessness of a schoolgirl reciting a poem from memory in front of a class, and the short, anxious breaths of a parent worried about a sick child. It includes the lung-expanding aerobic exercise of a ballet class or a long bicycle ride, and also the deep controlled breathing I learned in preparation for the birth of our two children. It includes coaching in public speaking and in singing, which helped me to use my breath more efficiently to produce vocal sounds. My history includes moments when the world and its beauty took my breath away. I have, so far, never been able to stifle a sudden gasp when I spy the crimson of the cardinal perched on the pine at the far edge of our garden. It also includes many sighs of relief when fears have been put to rest—when the lost child has finally been spotted in the crowded store, or when my husband has returned home safely on an icy night. Most of all, over the years my breath and my prayer have become so intertwined that, by quietly turning my attention to my breathing, I turn my attention Godward.

Turning my attention Godward has included times when I felt very close to God, who seemed as tangible as the oxygen that entered my lungs. But it has also included times when I felt starved for the assurance that God was indeed a presence in the world around me. Sometimes that meant I had neglected to breathe the deep draughts of prayer that I needed. But at other times, God's apparent absence seemed to have no cause. God just did not seem to be there, although in retrospect I realize God had been breathing in and through me constantly in what had seemed like emptiness.

My training as a dancer and musician and priest has taught me the importance of inhalation and exhalation, both as a metaphor for the life and rhythm of those professions and as a physical truth. The breath I share when making music or working or dancing or living with others has become a powerful image for me of the Spirit in the community of the people of God.

While one cannot actually *teach* others to pray, I have long believed that there are ways to provide guidance in creating an inner environment in which prayer can happen. Many of these ways involve preparation of the body, and in this area I must acknowledge my debts both to my training as a dancer and my exposure to eastern spiritualities. It seems strange indeed that a religion as incarnational as Christianity has been guilty of such a low regard for the body's part in spiritual growth, and I am grateful that in this respect the times are changing.

In the pages of *The Breath of God* you will find many different ways of praying and of integrating prayer and life. Use what helps you; gently release what does not. In offering variety, I hope never to suggest that one method of praying is any "better" than another. There will be times in our life when we need, for whatever reason, to call upon one particular way, but over the course of our life we will find occasion to use a great variety.

In each chapter, I will include suggestions about how each way of prayer can be "embodied," woven into the tapestry of daily life. It is in the unity of prayer and life that human wholeness and true holiness is found. This book is not primarily a book of "ways to pray" as much as a book about how to live fully as a human being.

At the end of each section, I have suggested prayer and breathing exercises. I hope that you will pray your way through this book slowly, for it is meant above all to draw out your own most natural ways of relating to God.

One of the reasons I wrote this book was so that I would have a textbook to offer participants in my own retreats and workshops about prayer. I hope that religious educators and spiritual guides will likewise find this book a useful resource for group prayer and discussion. It can also, of course, be used by individuals who wish to learn more about the Christian tradition of prayer and, even more, experience that tradition for themselves.

"The glory of God is the human being fully alive," St. Irenaeus wrote. The discovery that our prayer is as close to us as our inhalation and exhalation is an important step in our deepening friendship with God, whose breath gives us life. Just as we begin to yawn or gasp when our lungs lack oxygen, we begin to experience a vacuum when our lives lack prayer. I hope that this book will be a helpful companion in the expansion of your capacity for breath, for prayer, and for friendship with God, the provider of all: breath, prayer, and fullness of life.

Chapter One

Learning to Breathe Again

> Then the LORD God made an earthling from the earth, and breathed into its nostrils the breath of life; and the earthling became a living being. (Genesis 2:7)

This translation of the verse from Genesis is the most accurate way I can convey the fact that the passage contains a pun: the Hebrew word for human being—*adam*—derives from the word for earth—*adamah*. This one sentence of scripture is a distillation, in story form, of Hebrew belief about human

identity. When we understand this part of the book of Genesis
as theology conveyed through drama, we discover clues about
who we are and how we are meant to live and to pray.

We are earthlings, "of the earth, earthy." Whether we
think of the hand of God forming *adam* in Genesis from the
prehistoric *adamah* or "dust from the ground," or the mind
of God conceiving the evolution of human intelligence from
the primeval ooze of science's stories of beginnings, we know
from our own experience of life that we are bodies. From
infancy through old age, we are continuously reminded that
we are "dust." Our physical sensations—of hunger or satiety,
of illness or health, of fatigue or rest—all affect us profound-
ly. Religious teachings that urge us to despise or ignore our
bodies do not work for us. Our Hebrew ancestors believed
that God saw all creation, including the human body, as
good. The Christian faith proclaims God become flesh, the
Incarnation, as a central doctrine. Paul speaks of the body as
"the temple of the Spirit." There is no rationale in
Christianity for short-cutting the needs and wisdom of the
body in order to "move on" to things spiritual. The body
itself contains the capacity for holiness.

But we are more than our bodies. We have within us that
which is not *of* us: God's gift of breath. God breathes into our
nostrils the breath of life. God's breath enlivens the *adamah*
that is our physical selves, creating us as whole human beings.

If we think in these terms, we no longer can regard ourselves as two separate entities, "body" and "spirit," but as one: "bodyspirit." The Hebrews used the word *nefesh* to express the concept of bodyspirit, the unity of body brought to life by God's spirit. Looking at ourselves in this way, we cannot consider the body a burden and the spirit alone as good. Instead, we understand that the whole self is made holy to the extent we let God's spirit breathe in and through us. Our breath continues throughout our life in its inexorable rhythm, in and out. Inhalation, and exhalation. It reminds us of who we are: vessels of God's spirit, God-filled dust.

Prayer is the means whereby we let the Spirit of God breathe in and through us. As breath itself varies with our emotional and physical state, so our prayer varies. It can be a gasp for help, a groan of pain, the disciplined breathing of spiritual "exercises," sighs of longing, songs of joy, or the long, slow, deep breaths of contemplative prayer. Just as all kinds of inhalation and exhalation are breathing, all of these ways of "breathing the Spirit" are prayer.

Even emptiness itself is prayer, if we can permit ourselves to understand emptiness as part of the rhythm of the breath of God. In fact, the experience of emptiness can be one of our most powerful teachers, for it is a symptom of our desire for God. Just as our lungs crave oxygen and our whole body yearns for it if deprived of air for even a few moments, the human, *adam,* desires to be filled with God. "You have made us for yourself, and our hearts are restless until they rest in you," cried St. Augustine of Hippo in the fourth century. "Your life the Supreme Beneficence breathes forth and He enamours it of Himself so that it desires Him ever after," wrote Dante in the thirteenth century. "We are the hollow men," stated T. S. Eliot in the twentieth.

Emptiness is part of the human condition. It can produce despair or dependency, as well as desire for God. It is not comfortable to feel empty; it is difficult to accept those moments or even years when we do not *feel* as though we are filled with God. Because emptiness is uncomfortable, we often become frantic to fill the vacuum with such things as food, work, alcohol, or frantic activity. But the truth is that, even when we are not conscious of God's presence, God is there, holding us in life, breathing through us. We undermine our own well-being and stunt our growth by frantically filling the void. If our bodies and our lives are to become containers of the Holy, we must be content with the "exhalation times" as well as the "inhalation times" of our awareness of God.

The metaphor of the breath of God encompasses the whole Trinity. We need not equate God's enlivening breath with only the first person of the Trinity, for "in the beginning was the Word, and the Word was with God, and the Word was God " (John 1:1). The Word, Jesus Christ, breathes in us, at the center of our being. "The glory that you have given me I have given them, so that they may be one, as we are one, I in them and you in me," Jesus prayed as he took leave of his disciples (John 17:22-23). Paul sees Jesus Christ as a second *adam,* a man not of dust but from heaven, who himself "became a life-giving spirit" (1 Corinthians 15:45, 47).

The Holy Spirit, whose very name, *Spiritus,* means breath, breathes within us. In prayer, we breathe the divine energy of the Spirit and expand our consciousness of a world in sore need of the Spirit's vitality. We are "one in the Spirit," united in God to all other earthlings. We are united as well to our forebears in the faith, like the disciples who at Pentecost breathed the Spirit: "from heaven there came a sound like the rush of a violent wind, and it filled the entire house where they were sitting" (Acts 2:2).

At various times our temperaments, expectations, or needs may cause us to experience our prayer in relation to a specific person of the Trinity. Beyond those temporary perceptions, however, we are deepening our friendship with the whole Trinity as we learn to breathe the life of the Mystery we call God.

The metaphor of the breath of God helps us understand our experience of the Trinity, while affirming the fact that the Trinity *is* a mystery, in the sense of a truth beyond our rational comprehension. Like the air we breathe, God is invisible, yet we can experience God's action. We often find ourselves confused even about that, like the friend who once told me that when he was a child he was convinced that the *trees* made the wind because the wind only blew when trees were moving. God is beyond our comprehension, yet is the Source of our life. God is beyond our comprehension, yet loved us enough to become, in Jesus Christ, a second *adam*. God is beyond our comprehension, yet continues to hold us and the world in which we live in life. We can recognize God and God's action when we see the movement of love in the world, but we cannot "explain" God. Our best response to God's mystery is the response of our breath, bringing life to our prayer and prayer to our life.

Learning to breathe again may mean arranging our lives so that they contain a holy spaciousness. This endeavor is more a matter of changing our attitude than of altering our schedule. Most of us have more control over our expenditure of time than we admit. The restlessness that is born of our fear of emptiness causes us to fill our free moments with "usefulness." Part of the faith journey, as we mature, is finally to take full responsibility for our prayer, as we become fed up with our own excuses and opt for *living,* not partly living. A change of attitude occurs when we recognize that, despite our restlessness and fears, our higher priority in life is our deepening friendship with God. Paradoxically, it is this priority that gives zest and meaning to the activities and events in our day-to-day lives.

If we use the metaphor of breath to evaluate our daily, weekly, monthly, and yearly schedules, we will recognize that, no matter how important or worthwhile our outward activities, or "exhalations," we have a regular need for "inhalation" as well. While both inhalation and exhalation, as we shall see, are part of the rhythm of spiritual growth, most people neglect inhalation time. Look carefully at your days, weeks, months, and years to see if you can find a pattern of inhalation time that is appropriate to your life.

You need to be realistic about the possibilities. In looking at your daily schedule, for example, you may wish you could set aside an hour in the early morning, but since you are at home caring for young children, you may have only fifteen minutes during their afternoon naps. You may wish to spend a half-hour in a quiet church each day, but you may need to settle for the half-hour trip on the commuter train. Be clever and imaginative. It is very likely that your inhalation time is already there, waiting for you to discover it.

Look at your weekly schedule as well in order to discover a longer span of inhalation, perhaps one evening of prayer and study, or one long afternoon walk. If you can, plan periodic retreats, time alone in a place that nourishes your spirit. Many convents, monasteries, and retreat centers offer both silent retreats led by a retreat conductor and also the opportunity for individuals to visit on their own for a few days. But most of all, remember the many moments when, if only for a short while, you can pause and pay attention to your breath and the life of God within you.

You will also, especially in the beginning, need the breathing space of privacy in a place where you will be undistracted and uninterrupted. Your space may be the corner of a room, a *prie-dieu* in a small home chapel, a secluded ocean beach, or a grove in the woods. It may be your parish church, in the half-hour before a scheduled service begins. It may even be the space provided by the anonymity of public transportation—a train, subway, or bus.

Most of all, you need to find psychological breathing space, "thought space" during which you agree with yourself not to think about the pressure of other duties. With the human tendency to feel most worthwhile when we are busy, this may well be the most difficult space to find. But our thoughts need to breathe. We need to learn to let God be in control for a while, trusting the world will not come to a halt if we step aside for a moment from our duties.

In creating a holy spaciousness in your life, it is helpful to think of the time you spend in prayer as not merely a part of the day but as the *center* of the day, a center that nourishes you regularly with life-breath. Deepening our friendship with

God in prayer helps us remember God's presence in the world. Instead of being confused and scattered, we can go about our life's activities with what the Christian spiritual tradition calls "recollection," which literally means a collecting back together of all the pieces of ourselves. More than that, specific prayer time helps us to make life itself a prayer. It trains us to pay attention to God and teaches us how to move through our days with a consciousness of our friendship with God. Specific prayer times might be compared to training the pianist's fingers through learning scales and arpeggios in order to play a Mozart sonata, or training the ballerina's body through *barre* exercises in order to dance *Swan Lake,* or learning the grammar and vocabulary of a foreign language in order to speak it.

Spending regular time in prayer has a transforming effect not merely upon our attitude, but also upon our health. Medical research has demonstrated that learning to relax, breathe fully, and meditate can strengthen the immune system and help to counteract hypertension and high levels of cholesterol. Some scientists have even discovered that relaxation and meditation are more beneficial when undertaken in a faith context. That makes perfect sense to me because there would probably be little reason to relax without a God upon whom we could depend!

It is very good news indeed that prayer—the activity that calls us to fullness of life as Christians—also contributes to our health. But it should be no surprise, for if prayer is as natural to us as breathing, it should help us grow toward increased wholeness as human beings. It is no accident that the words for health, wholeness, and holiness spring from one Anglo-Saxon root, *hal*, and that they all refer to a state of being *together*, body and spirit, rather than divided.

In embarking on the adventure of prayer, we find a hidden treasure: our true identity as bearers of God's *ruach*. Prayer is not something we need to learn, but a matter of remembering who we are. This "re-membering," bringing together our dust and God's breath, is the way to life, as saints and mystics throughout the ages have told us. "The glory of God is the human being fully alive." To live and breathe the breath of God is the reason we were created. May these pages help you discover the Love who is as close to you as your life itself, as you remember how to breathe again the breath of God.

Breathing Space

When we were born, our entire body breathed: our bones, muscles, and organs moved with every breath. But by the time we are adults, sedentary living, tension, and tight clothing have caused most of us to forget how to breathe fully. Donna Farhi, the author of *The Breathing Book,* calls the way we breathed as young children the "essential breath." Breathing fully is not a matter of acquiring some new technique but rather, like prayer, it is a matter of "remembering."

Close your eyes. Try to breathe as you did as a child, not through controlling the breath in any way but through becoming once again, in your imagination, the child that you were. Imagine yourself as a newborn drawing your first breath. Then become a toddler making your first efforts at walking. Can you see yourself as an energetic three- or four-year-old playing in your yard or at the playground? Do you remember your healthy fatigue as you settled into bed each night and relaxed into slumber? What other breath memories do you have?

Offer God a prayer of thanks for your heart and lungs, which have served you well over the years.

For you yourself created my inmost parts;
  you knit me together in my mother's womb.
I will thank you because I am marvelously made;
  your works are wonderful, and I know it well.
My body was not hidden from you,
  while I was being made in secret
  and woven in the depths of the earth.[1]

PSALM 139:12-14

Chapter Two

The Breath and Preparation for Prayer

In learning to breathe again, we can begin, as did the Lord God in Genesis, with the raw material—*adamah,* or our physical selves. I have included here some suggestions for exercises that you can use in preparation for prayer; choose the ones you find helpful.[1] The important thing is to notice *adamah,* and to *use* the bodyspirit connection, not to disregard it.

Take time to notice how your body feels. Not only do we often drive the body to exhaustion, we ignore even the small signals to stretch, move, or relax. After sitting in one position for a period of time, as you have been while reading these pages, it is likely that you need to move.

EXERCISE

Stand and become aware of the weight of your body on the floor. Rock back and forth, and center your weight over the feet. Think of each foot as a tripod, made up of the heel, the pad of the big toe, and the pad of the little toe. Your weight should enter the ground just in front of the ankle. Try to align the body so that the hip joints are in a vertical line over the centers of the feet and the shoulder joints are over the hip joints. Then become aware of the counter-pull of the spine, stretching and reaching as if the tops of the ears were being pulled toward the sky. Standing tall like this enables you to breathe freely and reminds you of your connection to both heaven and earth.

Now inhale and let the arms float up in front of you and above your head. Reach with both arms toward the sky and, as you exhale, let them drop. Repeat this exercise a couple of times. Then, after you have dropped the arms to the sides, let the head fall forward. Feel the weight of the head become heavier and heavier, until your spine begins to relax toward the floor. It does not matter how far it relaxes. In fact, it does not matter if you omit this part of the exercise, if it is uncomfortable for you. You can even perform it seated in a chair. Let the body hang forward for a moment, then inhale and exhale, tighten the abdominal muscles, and slowly build up the spine, vertebra by vertebra, until you are erect again. When you are erect, check your alignment—shoulder joints over hip joints over the feet—and feel your ears being pulled up toward the sky.

Now, either in a standing or a seated position, drop the head forward, let it hang for a moment, and then lift it. Then let it drop toward the right shoulder, pause, and lift it again; repeat toward the left shoulder. Repeat the entire exercise a couple of times in order to stretch and relax the muscles of the neck.

Now stand (or sit) tall again, and raise the shoulders toward the ears. Pull them back, and let them drop. Pull them forward, up toward the ears again, then pull them back and let them drop. Repeat a few times and then reverse the circle. Much of our tension gathers in the neck and shoulder area, but you may have other points of tension you need to release through movement. Take some time to do so, and then take a position in which you will remain during your time for prayer.

POSITION FOR PRAYER

You may be most comfortable sitting in a straight-backed chair that gives the back support without letting it slump. Many eastern traditions suggest sitting in a cross-legged position for meditation, but this may be difficult if you are not accustomed to it, and inadvisable if you have any circulatory problems, although there are low meditation stools or cushions which can make that position more comfortable. There are many choices. You can sit on a pillow on the floor, with your back against a wall and your legs stretched out in front of you. Some people choose to lie down, but this position may make you become too sleepy. Kneeling and standing are probably not suitable for long periods, despite their common use in prayer. If these positions are meaningful for you, you may wish to use them for only part of your prayer time.

BREATHING

Now notice the ongoing rhythmic motion of your breath. Most adults use only a small part of their capacity to inhale and exhale. If you are instructed to take a deep breath, it is likely that your shoulders and upper chest rise, while the abdomen remains tight and immobile—just the opposite of the way we should breathe! Have you ever watched a baby breathe? As the infant lies on its back, the whole abdomen rises with each inhalation and falls with each exhalation. A baby has not yet built up the tensions that diminish respiration.

Learning to breathe properly is a time-honored tool in many spiritual traditions. It is easiest to learn lying on your back with the knees bent and the feet flat on the floor, although it is possible to do this exercise in a seated or standing position. Place your hands lightly on the lower abdomen, just below the navel. As you inhale, imagine that the air is actually going to the lower abdomen. If you wish, visualize a round balloon being filled with air. Permit the lower abdomen to rise as you inhale; then contract the abdominal muscles and press all the air out as you exhale. Practice this until it comes naturally. Do not overbreathe; this kind of breathing should feel natural and relaxed.

When you have learned abdominal breathing, move your hands up to the sides of the ribcage. If you have been visualizing a round balloon in the abdomen being filled with air, now picture an oval balloon that includes the ribcage. When the abdomen is "filled" with air, let the ribcage expand like a bellows. When you exhale, first "press the air" out of the abdomen and then let the ribcage fall. Practice this until it comes naturally.

Finally, let the whole torso, from the abdomen to the upper chest, become involved. Inhale and expand the abdomen and the ribcage, and then let the upper chest rise.

Exhale and press the air out of the abdomen, then let the ribcage and the upper chest fall. Try to breathe rhythmically, with the same number of counts on the inhalation and the exhalation. Do you feel now that you are taking a complete breath? Because you have released the abdominal muscles and the ribcage, the lungs are able to expand as they were intended to expand.

Experiment by breathing this way at different times during the day, particularly in stressful situations, and observing what happens to your mental state. You will notice that slow, deep breathing is extremely calming. No wonder that, in almost every spiritual tradition, the breath is associated with prayer. Just as oxygen, carried by the blood stream, revitalizes the whole body, so prayer revitalizes the whole human, *adam*.

RELAXATION

Take time to relax, slowly and deliberately, in any posture in which you can be comfortable while remaining alert. First, become aware of the weight of the body on the floor or chair. Now picture the tension draining from each part of the body in turn. You may need only to send a mental message, or you can move or tense each part of the body before you relax it, if that is helpful.

First picture the tension draining from the right foot, the right calf, and the right thigh. Then relax the left foot, the left calf, and the left thigh. Relax the buttocks, the abdomen, and the chest. Relax the muscles of the back and let all of the tension drain from the spine. Relax the right shoulder, the right upper arm, the right forearm, and the right hand. Relax the left shoulder, the left upper arm, the left forearm, and the left hand. Relax the front of the neck and the back of the neck. Relax the jaw, the cheeks, the area around the eyes, the area between the eyebrows, the forehead, and the scalp. Imagine that you are relaxing the inner organs of the body. The experience is one of releasing our usual tight muscular control and of learning to be at home with the quietness of body and of spirit that this progressive relaxation produces.

THE BODY AT PRAYER

These stretching, relaxing, and breathing exercises can be more than a preparation for prayer. They can become *in themselves* a way of prayer: the body at prayer. The act of stretching and becoming comfortable is a celebration of the goodness of the bodies that God created, an acceptance of *our* incarnation as well as an affirmation of *the* Incarnation. The very act of surrendering the tensions we carry in our bodies is a statement of trust in God, articulated through the body rather than through words. Breathing deeply and fully, especially as we come to associate that action with prayer, becomes an immediate reminder of God's presence.

There are many ways of stretching, relaxing, and attending to the breath. Find the ways you can best release the physical tension that can block God's breath in your life. Yoga is one way, a way I have explored in a Christian context in *An Invitation to Christian Yoga*. The exercise sequence known as Tai Chi is another. Some people find that aerobic exercise like swimming, cycling, or walking is helpful. Whatever methods of physical preparation for prayer you choose, the purpose is not competitive calisthenics but a gentle awareness of the body, the temple of the Spirit.

Breathing Space

Find a relaxed position and notice your breath. Then take your time to discover the answers to the following questions:

⤳ What parts of my body move when I breathe?

⤳ Is my breath fast, slow, or in between?

⤳ What is the rhythm of my inhalations and exhalations? Are they equal, or is one longer than the other?

↵ Is the texture of my breath even and smooth, or does it feel jerky and uneven?

↵ Is my breath deep or shallow? Does it feel as if I am using the full capacity of my lungs?

↵ What adjectives might I use to describe the quality of my breath (labored, light, constricted, free, anxious, calm)?

↵ What images might I use to describe my breathing (such as bellows fanning a fire, the rise and fall of ocean waves, a butterfly struggling and then resting, as it breaks out of its cocoon)?

In describing to yourself how you breathe, you are taking a baseline "x-ray." We begin any process of change, whether physical or spiritual, with the place we are. Perhaps, however, when you have reached the last pages of this book, some of your answers may have changed.

Now take some time to shift your attention, not to the physical act of breathing, but to the transforming of your breathing itself into prayer.

O Holy Spirit, by whose breath
life rises vibrant out of death;
come to create, renew, inspire;
come, kindle in our hearts your fire.

THE HYMNAL 1982, HYMN 501
ATT. RABANUS MAURUS (776-856)

Chapter Three

The Breath of God as Silence

Contemplative Prayer

Prayer is letting the Spirit of God breathe within us. It involves an ever-deepening companionship with the One who is with us in life and in eternity. The pattern of prayer can be compared to the nurturing of our companionship with other people who share our lives.

If we look at the pattern of our human relationships, we see that there are many ways in which our friendships grow and deepen. Sometimes we simply enjoy the presence of another person without any need for conversation. Sometimes a friend is very much in our thoughts. Sometimes we engage in lively conversation. And often our relationships are nurtured by working alongside our friends.

All these ways of deepening our human relationships—silence, thought, words, and action—have their parallels in our deepening companionship with God in prayer. The prayer of *silence* has traditionally been called "contemplative prayer" or "contemplation." The influence of eastern spirituality has made the terminology confusing, because in the east the selfsame activity is called "meditation." To further confuse the issue, the traditional Christian term for prayer as *thought* or "reflective" prayer has been either "discursive prayer" or "meditation." In short, "meditation" can have two different meanings! Communication with God through *words* has traditionally been called "verbal" or "vocal" prayer. Prayer as *action* implies carrying our prayer into our lives in what the French writer Jean-Pierre de Caussade called the "sacrament of the present moment": like the bread and wine of the eucharist, our lives themselves can be "outward and visible signs of inward and spiritual grace" (BCP 857).

In the past, many teachers of prayer taught that a person who was just beginning to pray should start with verbal prayer before moving on to a more "advanced" type of prayer: discursive, or reflective, prayer. Then, only when reflective prayer became impossible was one encouraged to approach God through contemplative prayer. These guidelines, while they may contain some truth, are, in my opinion, more suitable for the quieter era in which they were developed than for our time. In this chaotic and busy world, we may need, first of all, to learn the prayer of silence.

One of the factors that drew me to the teaching of prayer was the observation that my friends who were on personal spiritual journeys were journeying right out of the church into alternative spiritualities. It was in these other traditions that they found the teaching they desired on contemplative silence. It seemed to me that the church was hiding the treasure of her contemplative tradition. That contemplative tradition fills such a tremendous need for contemporary westerners that I believe it is helpful to learn at the very beginning of our prayer repertoire, rather than at the end, how to be silent in God's presence.

Most of us live in a world in which we are bombarded by stimuli. Traffic and airplane noise, the background hum of television and radio, and the vibrations of the machines that are supposed to make life more comfortable all ring in our ears. We are dizzied by images, particularly the stimulating media images trying to influence our buying habits. We hurry from one activity to another: both the inevitable busywork produced by ordinary daily life and the enjoyable activities we have chosen for ourselves. Ideas swirl around us. We know the national and international news as soon as it happens. We know what editors and commentators think about the news. We have thoughts of our own about the issues. Our choices today are so complex that we need to expend a great deal of energy in weighing options: what job to choose, whether to marry, whether to have children, where to spend our vacation, how to spend our evenings. It is a complicated, crowded, and confusing era in which to live, albeit an interesting one. No wonder that most of us often feel breathless.

Against the backdrop of a complex and fast-paced culture, the prayer of contemplation is like a deep breath that restores both body and spirit.

The prayer of the eastern traditions, the mechanics of which are taught in transcendental meditation or yoga meditation classes, has also been the prayer of the Christian saints and mystics. But it is not only for saints and mystics: it is a prayer for *all* earthlings! It has been called not only contemplative prayer, but "centering prayer" and "the prayer of silence." It involves not mere exterior silence, but interior silence. It is quiet attentiveness to God, characterized by the emptying of thoughts and words.

My favorite description of this kind of prayer is found in the story about a French parish priest who becomes curious about a peasant he notices praying for hours at a time in his little country church. One day, he finally interrupts him: "What are you doing all this time?" The peasant replies, pointing at the crucifix, "Why, it's very simple. I just look at Him, and He looks at me."

For some people at some times, it may indeed be very simple. For most of us, however, it is something we need to *learn*. When we try to "just look at God," we fall prey to innumerable distractions. As we try to focus on God, extraneous thoughts bubble up, flit by, crowd in, and make a general nuisance of themselves. Other traditions have described this state of distractedness as "monkey mind" or "mosquito mind." Contemplative prayer requires an environment of quiet, both of body and mind, and to achieve this we usually need some guidance.

A simple format for contemplative prayer includes *preparation, finding a focus,* and *passing beyond the focus.*

PREPARATION

Set aside time for your prayer, from fifteen minutes to a half hour. Take some time to exercise, stretch and relax the body, in whatever way suits you.

Find a prayer posture that suits you, and then take some time for attention to the breath. Breathe through the nostrils and let the breath "fill" the torso, including the abdomen, then exhale through the nostrils.

Now relax each part of the body in turn, beginning with the feet and continuing right up to the scalp. Let the chair or floor support you. Be at home with gravity; let yourself be an earthling. Let yourself also be at home with the quiet of body and mind that this exercise produces. This state of relaxed openness is the environment for contemplative prayer.

FINDING A FOCUS

The mind does not easily remain attentive to God. One needs to have a mental focus that guides one back to attentiveness when the inevitable distractions occur. Since we are so different from one another, each of us needs to experiment with the way we can best remain centered. Spiritual traditions have provided us with a variety of foci, including the breath, movement, a word or phrase, an image, and the senses of touch, hearing, taste, and smell.

The Breath

Attention to the breath may be all you need as a focus, especially if you tend to be very much in touch with your kinetic sense, or your sense of movement. You may simply pay attention to the movement of your body as you breathe, or to the sensation of the breath as it enters and leaves the nostrils. Or you may imagine you can watch the breath as it enters and leaves the body. A Zen abbot I know teaches his pupils to count breaths over and over again, from one to four, in order to remain focused. Whatever device you use, your focus on the breath is not merely on the interchange of oxygen and carbon dioxide, but on the rhythm of God's life moving in you and through you.

Movement

Repetitive movement is focusing for people who have a highly developed sense of the kinetic, and is probably helpful for *all* who wish to increase their sense of the bodyspirit connection. It is often used to accompany a chant. An example of a "movement mantra" is a pattern of simple arm movements accompanying a prayer to the Trinity: reaching upward as you address the Creator, out to the sides to form a cross as you meditate upon Jesus Christ, and bringing the hands inward toward the heart and then out again in reflecting upon the Spirit within and among us. You can create your own movement mantra, choosing a phrase to illustrate with a pattern of movement and then repeating that movement again and again.[1]

Improvisational dance-as-prayer is a broad area of celebrating bodyspirit, a topic that merits another book. When you wish to use improvisational movement in contemplative prayer, choose some music that appeals to you and then just move "before God," moving for the sake of the movement. It is "wordless movement," movement without concepts or form. This kind of movement is similar to the ecstatic or free-form that dance historians tell us was a primary form of worship among our ancestors. You can find it now in the dance of Sufi dervishes and in some African dance. It can be done at any tempo. I find that moving slowly to the haunting chants of David Hykes's Harmonic Choir is an experience of dancing contemplatively, letting myself just enjoy before God the movement of the body through space.

Various sports, such as running, swimming, walking, or cross-country skiing, lend themselves to the centering in which contemplative prayer takes place. You do not have to look far in sports literature to find testimonials to the holistic benefits of repetitive aerobic exercise.

A Word or Phrase
In many meditation systems, such as transcendental meditation, the teacher assigns a word, or mantra, upon which to focus. In Christian contemplative prayer, you may choose your mantra yourself. You may want to use a word that suggests the metaphor of God's breath, such as "God," or "holy," or "spirit." Or a phrase may be more helpful, espe-

cially one that matches the rhythm of your breath, such as "Come, Lord Jesus" or its Aramaic equivalent, *"Maranatha."* There are many phrases from scripture that are suitable for mantras, among them the sayings of Jesus in the gospels, such as "Fear not," or "I am the Way," and phrases from the epistles, such as "Know the love of Christ" or "Rooted and grounded in love" from the third chapter of Ephesians. The psalms are a treasure-trove of mantras, such as "Be still, and know that I am God!" (Psalm 46:10) and "His steadfast love endures forever" (Psalm 118:29).

The desert tradition, which we can trace to those monks who sought a purer form of religion than was possible in the secular world after the adoption of Christianity by Constantine in the fourth century, has given us the most frequently prayed mantra in Christianity: the Jesus Prayer. The Jesus Prayer, still widely practiced by Eastern Orthodox Christians, is prayed in conjunction with the breath and the heartbeat. It is said that this mantra becomes so second-nature that it bestows upon the one who prays the gift of *hesychia,* or inner peace. The complete form of the Jesus Prayer is "Lord Jesus Christ, Son of God, have mercy on me, a sinner," but it is often shortened to "Jesus, mercy," or merely "Jesus."

If you use a mantra as a focus, remember that its use is a means, not an end. The point is *not* to become proficient at focusing on a mantra; instead, the mantra is like a doorway through which we gaze at our true focus, God. Like a doorway, it provides a framework for our attention. What we enter through this doorway is not the outside world, but the inside world, at the center of which beats the unending rhythm of God's life in us.

Contemplation is no mere exercise of the intellect. It is an exercise of love. The anonymous author of the fourteenth-century treatise *The Cloud of Unknowing* advised his pupils to use a short repetitive word or phrase to "shoot a dart of longing love" through the cloud of unknowing beyond which is the infinite mystery of God. The mantra is our arrow, a way of directing love toward God.

An Image
An image is helpful as a focus for people who are visually oriented. A visual focus may be an outward image upon which one gazes, as in the example of the peasant looking at the crucifix. Many find a candle flame compelling, as they focus on the Light both beyond us and within us. A beautiful scene from nature, a statue, or a painting all can be windows through which we gaze at the God beyond all images. The use of icons in the Orthodox tradition illustrates the concept of an image as a window: the icon is believed to reveal the reality beyond it. You may have noticed that in the background

of some icons is a kind of reverse perspective, with the distant background larger in scale than the near background. This is meant to suggest that the holy world into which we are gazing is more vast than the one in which the observer stands.

I have on my bookshelf a beautiful small volume, *The Quiet Eye: A Way of Looking at Pictures,* by Sylvia Shaw Judson, which draws me into interior silence when I merely look at its cover. The author, a Quaker, has chosen masterpieces from many eras of art history, from a Greek urn to a sketch by Henry Moore, which are juxtaposed with short texts that are in themselves like mantras. In seeking her images and texts, she writes that she wanted

to find examples with a sense of "divine ordinariness," a delicate balance between the outward and the inward, with freshness and a serene wholeness and respect for all simple first-rate things, which are for all times and all people.[2]

Using those guidelines, you may wish to find your own "quiet eye" paintings or objects, either from art or from nature, upon which to gaze as you contemplate the Artist who inspires all art.

On the other hand, you may find your mind quieter if you close your eyes and visualize an image or scene. It may be a religious image, such as a crucifix or your own picture of

Jesus, or a landscape or interior that gives you a sense of the
numinous. The sea, mountains, cathedrals, forests, chapels,
gardens, indeed almost every space on earth can be a con-
tainer and revealer of the Spirit, depending on our associations with them. I remember leading a workshop in seminary
in which I had participants visualize a rural scene in which
they felt the presence of God. Afterward, a classmate moved
us all by speaking about finding God's presence surrounding
her on the busy city streets where she had grown up. On the
other hand, I will never forget a pupil's vivid description of
the divine presence he felt as a young boy when he lay in the
rich dirt of his father's tomato patch, looking up at the blue
sky through the jungle of green leaves. Think of where *you*
have most experienced a sense of the holy, and try to be present there again in your imagination.

You can add meditative drawing to the focus of seeing.
The act of really *seeing* a scene or object and letting pencil,
pen, or brush respond to it is a contemplative focus for artist
and non-artist alike. Frederick Franck speaks of "seeing/draw-
ing" so that the pencil point becomes like a "seismographic
needle that registers the inner tremors."[3] Franck's books, *The
Zen of Seeing* and *The Awakened Eye,* are useful companions
for those who find that actually drawing, rather than merely
gazing, brings clarity of mind and spirit and a sense of God's
presence.

The Sense of Touch

The sense of touch can provide a very powerful focus. Holding an object uses one of our earliest developed senses; have you noticed how an infant discovers the world? Hold a round stone, a shell from the beach, a small crucifix, a rosary, even a blade of grass in the palm of your hand, and explore the object with the sense of touch. How heavy is the object? What is its texture? Can you discern its shape? How does it feel against the palm? Against the fingertips? Against the cheek? Like the icon or image for visualization, the object you hold becomes a window for God. Cradling the object, you can feel your unity with creation or to the reality that object represents, and, through that window, your unity with the Creator. I suggest that you gather together a collection of objects you can use in this way.

I do not mean to belittle the tactile focus for contemplative prayer when I compare it to the beloved blanket to which so many of us clung as very young children. Do you remember the immediacy of the comfort it bestowed? If you habitually make use of an object that reminds you of God, you are enriching your prayer by using your important capacity to train the mind to make habitual associations.

The Sense of Hearing

The aural sense is also very powerful in its ability to draw our attention toward God, for music reaches a level of consciousness deeper than any words can reach. Music that speaks to you of God's presence creates, paradoxically, a deep silence within the mind and heart as you open yourself to the rhythm of God's breath within. You need to discover for yourself what kind of music leads you to inner harmony. I myself turn to Bach when the disordered world within me or without needs ordering, and it is no coincidence that Bach inscribed all of his music *soli deo gloria*—"to God alone be glory." Plainchant, with all its associations with the age of faith, is another wonderful expression of the contemplative in music, as are the chants and antiphons composed by Jacques Berthier for the contemporary ecumenical community of Taizé. For me, also, the music of the French composer and organist Olivier Messiaen is unique in its ability to draw me into the reality of God's presence. It is, in the words of T. S. Eliot, "music heard so deeply that it is not heard at all, but you are the music while the music lasts."[4]

There are also recordings of environmental sounds—ocean, rain forest, meadow, mountain stream—that can create a quiet sound environment for your prayer focus. Or you can, very simply, listen to the sounds that actually surround you. At this moment, for example, I hear a spectrum of sounds: the low hum of the computer and the rhythm of my fingers on the keys, a bird calling out, a car passing, a dog barking, an airplane overhead, the high whine of crickets, the voices of children playing. Just sitting and focusing on these sounds, as if they were a kind of environmental symphony, can help to produce a state of inner harmony. We used to do this exercise in my meditation class at Manhattan Plaza, which happens to be located at the corner of 42nd Street and 9th Avenue in New York City. There, environmental sounds included the sirens of fire engines and ambulances, the screech of brakes, automobile horns, loud conversations, and the air conditioning fan; even there, listening to sounds as vibrations rather than as intrusions served as an excellent focus.

Singing or chanting also comes under the heading of "sound." Augustine of Hippo wrote that a singer "prays twice." In singing, as in speaking, the breath is exhaled past the vocal cords to produce audible vibrations. When singing, however, we use more of the body's energy than we do when speaking. When singing, we can feel the music vibrating in our bodies. As we take our individual parts in producing sound, we can feel deeply in touch with the One who gives us the breath to sing.

Perhaps you play a musical instrument and know the focus that comes through pure attention to the music you produce. You can direct that attention to God by "aiming" it, like the arrow in *The Cloud of Unknowing,* before your music-making begins, and then losing yourself in the music. Many musicians have expressed their sense of finding themselves by losing themselves in their music, which surely could be a description of authentic contemplative prayer.

The Sense of Smell

The part of the brain that registers the sense of smell is, I am told, immediately adjacent to the place where memories are stored. If you have associations with particular fragrances that remind you of the holy, you may wish to use fragrance in preparation for prayer and as a centering device. The sense of smell is perceived, of course, through breathing, so there is an additional powerful connection with prayer.

If you have visited an ashram—a religious meditation center—you know that the smell of incense usually pervades the room used for meditation. In the Christian church, incense has been used by worshipers over the centuries to symbolize their prayers rising toward God. If you associate the fragrance of incense with a sense of the holy, you may wish to burn some in the place where you pray.

There are other fragrances, such as fresh pine needles or salt sea air, that also remind us of God's presence in the world. I once even had a pupil who confessed that the fragrance of her favorite soap so calmed her that she would always take some time to breathe its perfume as she began to meditate!

The Sense of Taste
Taste, like smell, has the capacity to evoke memories, and thus can be a helpful focus from time to time. A slice of home-baked bread, eaten slowly, for example, can remind us of the comfort not only of a mother's kitchen, but also of a God who provides our daily bread as well as our breath. Bread and wine, after all, were Jesus Christ's choice of a window to God for us, and we should not overlook the focus they provide.

Exploration
We are all so different from one another that some of the above suggestions will appeal to you more than others. Explore the ones that help *you* center your attention on God; no doubt you will also discover other ways of focusing your prayer as you begin to pray.

Take advantage of the change of seasons in exploring foci for contemplative prayer. In the spring, find a spring bulb in flower and let that sight and its fragrance be your window to God. If you live in a city, notice the new buds on the trees planted along the sidewalk. In the summer, let the warmth of sunshine on your skin or the coolness of a glass of ice water, sipped slowly, draw you to the point of stillness in God's presence. In the autumn, pick up a crimson leaf or a pinecone. In the winter, let the sunlight reflected on the snow or the clear night sky speak to you of God's light shining in the darkness.

PASSING BEYOND THE FOCUS

There may come a time when you can drop the focus you have chosen and just *be,* silent in God's presence. When that happens, do not struggle to maintain the focus. When God's presence itself becomes your focus, it is not your own accomplishment. It is God praying through you. At those moments, permit yourself to just *be,* in the present, in the experience. Do not try to analyze the experience; try to set aside the part of you that observes and evaluates, so that you do not distance yourself by commenting mentally on the experience.

The focus you use might be compared, in fact, to a raft that carries you over a lake to a beautiful meadow on the other side. Once you have reached that meadow, you no longer need to stay on the raft. As you grow in the use of contemplative prayer, it may be that sometimes you only need to sit down, relax, and notice your breath for a moment in order to have a sense of God's near presence. At other times, you may come to prayer distracted and fragmented and will need the structure that a focus like one of the above provides. It is more usual than not that distractions will occur. There is a delightful story told about Teresa of Avila, a great teacher of prayer, in which one of her novices comments to her enviously that it must be wonderful to have no distractions in prayer. Teresa is said to have replied, "What do you think I am: a saint?"

It is best, therefore, to think of this prayer of "just looking at God" as a continual process of learning. When intruding thoughts occur—what you are going to buy for dinner tonight or what you said to your sister yesterday—do not fight the distractions but let them pass by, like birds flying across the horizon, and then gently re-focus. You have probably had the experience of talking with one person at a crowded party where many other conversations were going on. You attempt to focus on that one person with whom you are conversing, despite the fact that from time to time extremely interesting conversational snatches from elsewhere come your way. So you already know the process of how to deal with distractions in contemplative prayer. Be gentle and understanding with yourself. And if an idea comes during prayer that you do not wish to lose, jot it down and then dismiss it until after your quiet time is over.

During your prayer time, you may be disturbed to discover negative thoughts and feelings. Perhaps they seem like dark corners from the past, corners that have not been brought to the light of consciousness for a long time. Or they may be, instead, current resentments or other emotions of which you had not been aware. You need not fear these thoughts and feelings. They are part of the *adamah,* the "dust" of our human life. Rather than being alien material, these negative thoughts represent a part of your life in particular need of God's life and love. When these thoughts and feelings occur, imagine that you are holding the "negative dust" in your hands before God for a moment before going back to your meditation focus. If you need to, you can write down the problem that is disturbing you, with the intention of returning to it after your time of prayer. If you cannot return to your meditation, you may wish to use the image of holding the dust before God's transforming love the *focus* of your meditation.

Especially with this mode of prayer, sleepiness may be a problem for you. Two physical adjustments may help: keeping your eyes half-open but unfocused, and making sure that your spine remains straight. If you still doze off, you may need to find another time of day for your prayer time.

In contemplative prayer, there is very little immediate sense of accomplishment. At the time, it usually seems as if one is doing nothing. That is one reason, I believe, that we both yearn for this kind of prayer and also sometimes resist it. There seems to be a lack of purposefulness about it that does not correspond to our ideas of how a useful person should spend time. "Wasting time with God" falls into the same category as a child's daydreaming, an adolescent's dawdling, or an adult's lack of initiative.

The reality is that, although contemplative prayer seems to be purposeless, it accomplishes more than we will ever know, in terms of both the world in which we live and our own interior growth. The world is, in fact, probably held together by contemplation rather than by politics! A group of Roman Catholic sisters were sent, for example, to a strife-torn city in Central America to found a convent in the middle of the violence—and pray! They were there to be attentive and open to God on behalf of those around them who were warfare's perpetrators and victims, to breathe the life of God in the midst of death and destruction. The power of contemplative prayer to transform the world is not obvious; it is the power of the subtle but steady impact of goodness on the course of events.

The power of contemplative prayer to transform the one praying is a familiar story in the lives of Christian saints, but it has also been noted in very ordinary people—if such a thing as an "ordinary" person exists! The psychologist Lawrence LeShan writes of the meditator's growing ability to attend to one thing at a time in daily life as well as in the time of meditation:

> It is the steady work in which one gently, firmly and
> consistently brings oneself back to the task at hand that
> strengthens the will, purpose, goal-oriented behavior,
> ability to bar distractions, etc., and facilitates the per-
> sonality reorganization that is part of our slow, endless
> growth to real maturity.

LeShan also notes that a different viewpoint toward the
world begins to emerge, a new way of perceiving and relating
to reality:

> We also begin to *know* that each of us is a part of all
> others, that no one walks alone, and that we are indeed
> at home in, and a part of, the universe.[5]

It is the steady work of learning contemplative attentiveness that prepares us psychologically for such a perception.
The scholar Joseph Campbell, in writing about this sense of
unity with the universe, says that the difference between the
experience of a person who has prepared through contemplation and a person who plunges into a "mechanically induced
mystical experience" through hallucinogenic drugs is like the
difference between a deep sea diver who can swim and one
who cannot.[6]

In neurobiological language, we quiet the babble of
thoughts produced in the brain's left hemisphere in contem-

plation, in order to spend time in the right hemisphere. Through this shift of brain activity, we open not merely our conscious mind but also our unconscious to the transforming power of God. No wonder that such prayer, although it seems like "doing nothing," produces transformed lives. The metamorphosis occurs at a level far below the surface of awareness, as old habits are changed and old hurts are healed. As LeShan points out, both the psyche and the world-view are transformed. We learn to see each person, each tree, each patch of blue sky as a wonder worthy of awe. We are also likely to become more sensitive to the needs of the earth community. When we comprehend the truth that "each of us is a part of all others... and that we are indeed at home in, and a part of, the universe," we can begin to move out of our accustomed egocentricity and anthropocentricity. Our desire for the reconciliation of the human family and for the well-being of the earth, which we share with the rest of God's creatures, becomes more compelling.

Contemplative prayer nurtures contemplative living, as we learn to live fully in each moment. Living fully in the present moment is a singular characteristic of the saints and mystics of all religions, who perceive holiness in the ordinariness of daily life. The quiet focus that we learn in contemplative prayer can be transferred to a focus on the tasks at hand, whatever they may be. The sense of "center" built up through this prayer is carried within us, giving us stability in God as we move through our days. The patron saint of this kind of living may well be the humble monastery cook Brother Lawrence, who, it is said, was "never hasty or loitering, but did every thing in its season, with an even, uninterrupted composure and tranquillity of spirit." Indeed, he admitted that

> the time of business does not with me differ from the time of prayer, and in the noise and clatter of my kitchen, while several persons are in the same time calling for different things, I possess God in as great tranquillity as if I were upon my knees at the Blessed Sacrament.[7]

I remember, in my twenties, being struck by the title of the Quaker writer Douglas Steere's book *On Being Present Where You Are,* in which he teaches about the centeredness that comes from living in the present moment.[8] Contemplative living is indeed focused on the *now;* it is the unself-conscious absorption in the task at hand that we can observe—and envy—in the children we know. It is a way of living, however, that we can begin to learn as we practice the prayer of contemplation.

What if you find this way of prayer difficult? It is important to recognize that this way of praying is not for all people at all times and in all places. If you find becoming quiet mentally and physically frustrating, you might review the section in this chapter on using movement as a focus, and incorporate contemplation with a regular exercise regimen, such as running, cycling, or swimming. Or you might turn to some of the ways of praying in the next chapters of this book. Even those people who find contemplative prayer most natural experience times when the emptiness of contemplation may not be the most helpful way to pray, especially in times of crisis or tragedy. At those times, imaginative reflective prayer using scripture, or verbal prayer, either spoken or written in a journal, may be the way we need to direct our attention toward God breathing into the *adamah* of our lives.

Still, I have placed contemplative prayer first: I am convinced that we all have the capacity for being with God in this way, and that indeed some people have been with God in this way their whole lives and have never realized it was prayer. I suspect that our true prayer as children was contemplative, even before we learned about the concept of God. That is perhaps why, time after time, people who have discovered this way of relating to God—whether it be the contemplation taught by the saints and mystics of the church or the meditation taught in courses on spiritual development—have exclaimed, "Why, it's just like coming home!"

Breathing Space

1. In contemplative prayer we become aware of our inner selves, strengthening our ability to let God breathe into the very center of our being. In many of the world's spiritual disciplines, the center of the body—a place a couple of inches below the navel—is seen as the source of our strength and our life. Strengthening that "core" and breathing from it can have a direct relation to our prayer.

Lie on your back with the knees bent and feet flat on the floor. You will notice that there are natural curves in the spine, and that the small of the back does not touch the floor. Inhale. Now exhale and contract the abdominal muscles inward and upward, as if you were zipping up a pair of slacks or lacing up a hiking boot. Imagine that you can press your navel against your backbone. Hold the contraction for a few seconds, then relax and take a deep breath, letting the abdomen rise and fall.

A variation of this exercise involves increasing the contraction so that you are actually pressing the small of the back into the floor as you exhale.

"Abdominal breathing" helps us increase our ability both to expand our "core" and to build its strength. Strong abdominal muscles give support to our spines, lessening the risk of back injury as we move about our daily lives. In a similar way, breathing fully the *ruach* of God builds our strength to lead courageous and meaningful lives.

2. We are usually not conscious that there is a short pause after each of our exhalations. It is a kind of physical "sabbath," a time of rest that helps us become open and receptive to the next breath.

Find a position in which you can relax completely, either sitting in a chair or lying down with the knees bent and feet flat on the floor. Listen to the sound of the breath and feel the sensation of the breath, noticing your inhalations and exhalations.

Now begin to focus more and more on your exhalation. Follow the exhalation to the very last whisper of the breath. Notice that there is a short pause at the end of each breath. The next inhalation is born of this moment of stillness.

Focus on this pause, letting yourself surrender to the moment of emptiness. Notice that the new breath arises without any effort on your part. As you continue, you will probably discover that the pause becomes more spacious. Allow yourself to rest in this moment.

As you go about your life after this exercise, remember that you carry the peace of this stillness within you, for it is a sign of God, "the breath inside the breath."[9] We need only to notice the breath, the reminder of the Source of light, love, and life, closer to us than our very selves, yet also the eternal mystery beyond us, whom we know—and seek—throughout our human journey.

You are the seeker's sure resource,
of burning love the living source,
protector in the midst of strife,
the giver and the Lord of life.

HYMN 501, VERSE 2

Chapter Four

The Breath of God as Thought

Reflective Prayer

As we look at the ways that prayer, the breath of God, can transform us, I am reminded of the nineteenth-century Russian bishop Theophan's description of prayer as "standing before God with the mind in the heart." In eastern thought, the "heart" refers not merely to the emotions but to the whole person—emotions, body, imagination, intellect, and will. Theophan was saying that prayer transforms our entire being, not merely those parts of us that we might think of as "spiritual," such as the mind or the emotions.

In reflective prayer, our thought processes are directed toward God and opened to God. These thought processes are not merely intellectual, but engage the whole "heart," understood as our emotions, body, imagination, intellect, and will. Reflective prayer is thinking with all that we are, including the senses: touch, taste, smell, sight, hearing. It is an opening of the unconscious as well as the conscious mind. We need to reclaim and deepen this kind of prayer, because the separation of faith and intellect has been one of the more troublesome divisions in our dualistic culture.

Reflective prayer has a long history because, like the prayer of contemplation, it is a natural capacity of the human being. The psalmist exults, "Oh, how I love your law! It is my meditation all day long.... How sweet are your words to my taste, sweeter than honey to my mouth!" (Psalm 119:97, 103). Notice that the use of the sense of taste in these lines indicates that God's word is delicious nourishment for the *whole* self. Pious Jews have meditated on the Torah—God's law and the sacred history of God's people—for centuries.

In the Christian spiritual tradition, Saint Benedict, the founder of western monasticism, taught his monks to spend four hours a day in *lectio divina* ("divine reading") during which they were to "ruminate" on scripture. The word

Benedict used, *ruminare,* is the word used for a cow chewing its cud! The monk was to read slowly, at his own pace, letting a few words at a time sink deep into his heart. If he could not read, he listened to another monk reading the passage long enough for him to remember and ruminate on the text. Rumination brought together mind and heart, as the meaning of the words sank deep into the consciousness. The monk spent time in silent prayer and then continued the rhythm of reading (or listening), rumination, and silence.

During the Counter Reformation, Ignatius of Loyola, the founder of the Society of Jesus, recorded in his *Spiritual Exercises* a similar discipline of reflection on scripture. Ignatius's format was more detailed than Benedict's, but his intention was the same: to engage the whole capacity of the human mind in the venture of prayer. He advised careful preparation for prayer, both in advance and at the time of prayer. A prayer for God's blessing preceded the reading of a passage of scripture, which was usually a vivid story from the gospels. The monk then used his imagination to visualize the passage in detail, and his "memory, intellect, and will" to reflect on what the passage meant in terms of transformation of life. Finally, the monk made a "resolution" to express in action what he had learned in prayer, and prayed for grace to keep this resolution. For example, a brother who felt he had been hard-hearted toward his neighbor would resolve to pray

for him, as well as to pay special attention to his neighbor's
well-being.

I have found it helpful to simplify Ignatius's format by
using four words beginning with the letter "P": *prepare, picture, ponder,* and *permit.* Set aside at least twenty minutes for
this exercise, so that you will not feel hurried.

PREPARE

Preparation ideally includes choosing and reading the passage the night before as well as again at the time of prayer. In
that way, the images in the passage can be "simmering on the
back burner" as you sleep. It is best, especially at the beginning, to choose a story or parable that you will be able to
picture easily.

At the time of prayer, take time for whatever physical
preparation you need. Find a position in which you can relax,
and note the weight of the body and the movement of the
breath. Spend some time "watching" the breath enter and
leave the nostrils; picture your exhalations cleansing your
mind of distracting worries, and your inhalations bringing
you the peace and wisdom of God's *ruach.* Then quietly lift
up the prayer time to God and read the passage again. This
preparation time helps you to begin in the spirit of prayer, so
that you can truly *attend* to the words you read.

PICTURE

Now read the passage again slowly, picturing as many details as possible. Use the "eyes" of the imagination. Visualize the setting: the landscape, buildings, and sky. Visualize the people in the story. What can you learn about them through the expressions on their faces or the way they used their bodies? If you have access to a biblical commentary or other study resource, so much the better. The more you know about the historical, social, and literary background of the story, the richer your picture will be. For example, when visualizing the scene in the parable of the Good Samaritan, find out all you can about that dangerous and dusty road to Jericho. Learn what the rules were for priests and Levites, and why Samaritans were considered outcasts by faithful Jews.

Then use your other senses. Use the "ears" of the imagination: what sounds would you have heard if you had been there? The crashing of waves against a boat in the story of Jesus' stilling of the storm? The hum of insects and of conversation amidst the green grass in the story of the feeding of the five thousand?

Use your other senses imaginatively. How would those loaves and fishes have tasted, as you satisfied the gnawing hunger in your stomach after a long hot day? How would the bread and wine, accompanied by Jesus' strange and bittersweet words of farewell, have tasted in the upper room in Jerusalem?

Do not forget the sense of smell: the salt air of the Sea of Galilee, the stench of the crowds surging along the Way of the Cross, the sweetness of the ointment poured over Jesus' feet.

And remember the sense of touch. Can you imagine the hot sun on your skin, the coarse nets of the fishing boats, the water lapping against your ankles in the story of the calling of the brothers Simon and Andrew? The bone-chilling waves in the story of the stilling of the storm? The feel of Jesus' touch on your eyelids in the story of the healing of the blind men?

Now use the kinetic sense. Either actually move or move in your imagination through some of the actions of the story. In "picturing" the story of Mary and Martha, first move as if you were Martha, distracted and overburdened, trying to prepare dinner for an honored guest and a lazy sister. Do you feel the tension and fatigue in your body? Now "become" Mary, sitting quietly at Jesus' feet, focused totally on his words. What is the difference in the quality of your breathing, as you become each sister in turn?

Or become the bent woman unable to straighten herself for eighteen years who, touched by the strong hands of Jesus, was freed from her infirmity. Become the disciples in Gethsemane, limbs numb with fatigue and eyelids heavy with sleep, or the fleet-footed messengers of joy on the morning of the resurrection.

"Picturing," although it is a visual word, thus becomes visceral, engaging every sense in the exploration of scripture. By entering a story in this way, you are respecting the passage as it is in itself before moving on to the next step: pondering what the story means to you.

PONDER

Ponder is a beautiful word, sharing its root—the Latin *pondus,* meaning "weight"—with words like "ponderous" and "pendulum." Pondering the passage means letting its weight sink deeper and deeper into us, until it speaks to our hearts. In pondering a passage, hold the scene before God, asking God to help you understand the "weight" of the passage for you. Perhaps only a word or phrase will speak to you. Perhaps one of the characters will stand out in high relief. Perhaps the passage will stir up a vivid memory. Or perhaps you will hear a question.

Take your time. Let your mind feel relaxed and open, so that the passage can touch you deeply, beyond your conscious mind. By using all the capacities of the conscious mind during your period of "picturing," you have prepared for this time of contemplative listening. This is a part of the prayer that may well continue long after you finish your period of prayer time.

Instead of Ignatius's word "resolution" I prefer the word "permit," which conveys a kind of cooperation between God and the one who prays. For me, "permit" asks the question: "How will I *permit* the breath of God to breathe more completely through me as a result of this meditation?"

This part of your reflective prayer is the bridge that connects the time of prayer and daily life. It can consist of a simple symbolic action—anything from making a long-overdue telephone call to praying for God's reconciling love to enter a particular international crisis. Or it may be a more dramatic action, even a change in your style of life. Perhaps, for example, you have meditated on the story of Jesus' feeding of the five thousand as told in the sixth chapter of John's gospel, and you have been struck by the action of the boy who gave his lunch away—five barley loaves and two fish. The child's actions made you see your acquisitiveness in a different light, and you resolved to practice being more generous by sharing some of your possessions with others.

This part of the prayer, like *pondering,* is listening time. Do not become anxious about producing a resolution or "permit action." If nothing comes to you after some time of quiet and listening, simply let this part of the prayer be an offering of your life's activities to God during the day ahead.

Finally, conclude your meditation by giving thanks to God for this time of being in God's presence.

≈≋

This pattern of *prepare, picture, ponder,* and *permit* may be used with readings other than scripture. Literature that lends itself to such prayer might include Dante's *Divine Comedy,* the writings of the mystics, and devotional and theological classics. But literature need not even be overtly religious in nature to be used as a basis for reflective prayer. We each have our own favorite literary modes through which God can speak to us. I particularly enjoy published letters and journals—everything from Friedrich von Hügel's *Spiritual Counsel and Letters* to Anne Truitt's *Daybook: The Journal of an Artist*—and find that they broaden my understanding of God's action in people's lives. By the same token, I have friends who find that fiction enriches their reflective capacity.

Content for reflective prayer need not even appear in written form. An incident in your life, your dreams, a work of art, or a natural object all can be foci for such prayer. As you become familiar with praying in this way, you will, no doubt, discover other foci, in addition to the suggestions that follow.

AN INCIDENT IN YOUR LIFE

Reflective prayer is a way to *use* rather than to dismiss thoughts about a recent event in your life or an incident from the past. The focus of your time of reflective prayer could be a relatively trivial encounter with a shopkeeper, a joyous event in your family, an unsettling confrontation with an employer, or even a difficult international situation.

Prepare

Is there an incident that you cannot get out of your mind? One good way to identify such an incident is by asking yourself the question, "What keeps you awake at night?" Several years ago, a friend of mine found herself sleepless because of unjust accusations made by a colleague. She decided to take the situation before God in reflective prayer.

Once you have identified the incident about which you wish to pray, take some time for preparation of body and mind through relaxing, breathing, and centering.

Picture

Then relive the incident in as much detail as possible. You may wish to write it down, or to reread what you have already written in a journal. Relive not merely the outward event, but how it made you *feel*. If other people were involved, try to imagine their thoughts and emotions. In reliv-

ing her encounter with her colleague, my friend saw once
again her colleague's angry face, heard her cold voice, and felt
once again her own pain and frustration because of her
inability to convey the truth of the situation.

Ponder

Now hold the incident before God, asking for help in hearing
God's voice through the event. Let the incident speak to you.
What does it reveal to you about yourself? About your
strengths, your weaknesses, your goals, or your limitations?
About your relationship to God, to others, to yourself, and to
the world? There is nothing, absolutely nothing, in our lives
that cannot become a "teacher" by revealing something valu-
able to us—even things that at the time seemed destructive
and painful.

Remember that you are looking at this incident *in the light
of God,* whose way of being with us in the world is the way
of resurrection from death. If the incident is a painful one, let
the resurrection light dawn. If the incident is joyous one, let it
shine even more brightly. When my friend pondered the incident that distressed her, she found herself wondering what
difficulties in her colleague's past caused her behavior and
began to have compassion toward her. She also found herself
wondering why her colleague's false accusations had so much

power over her and became aware of her desire to please others that sometimes was unhealthy.

Permit

What does the incident suggest to you in the way of action? Perhaps the "permit" is a giving up of a long-harbored grudge, now that you have gained some understanding of another person's emotions and motivations. In my friend's situation, she recognized the necessity of permitting God to heal her painful memory of the encounter and also was drawn to pray for her colleague's well-being. Whatever our response, our decision embodies our acceptance of the rhythm of resurrection from death that is the reality of our life in God.

End with a moment of quiet and gratitude for the gift of life, with all the experiences that it brings to you.

A NATURAL OBJECT

I have found that reflection about a natural object is one of the most powerful ways of connecting the mind and the heart in prayer. Objects from nature frequently evoke in us an awe that we have not experienced since we were children discovering the world and its wonders. Awe opens us to God's presence in a unique way. Natural objects contain an innate wisdom for, unlike us, they are consistently true to their own natures. Earth's messages come through loud and clear. These

messages are often extremely helpful to earthlings who sometimes resist the inevitable rhythms of earthly life.

Prepare

Choose an object from nature, such as a shell, a rock, a twig,
or a pinecone. You may wish to begin your prayer time by
taking a walk outdoors in order to find a small natural object
that attracts your attention. On the other hand, you may
already have a collection of objects. A friend, knowing that I
enjoy collecting small rocks as souvenirs of my travels, gave
me one of my favorite objects for meditation: a stone polished
smooth by the waves of the sea of Galilee.

Now prepare your bodyspirit, holding the object in the
palm of your hand as you relax.

Picture

As with the other foci for meditation, picturing your object
involves more than the sense of sight. First, imagine that you
possess *only* the sense of touch. Close your eyes and concen-
trate on feeling the object. Is it rough or smooth? Prickly or
soft? Light or heavy? How does it feel against your hands?
Your fingers? Your cheek?

Now use only your sense of hearing. Does the object make
any sounds? Shake it. Tap it.

Does it have any fragrance? Or—if the object is something like a piece of fresh bread—what does it taste like?

Now open your eyes and look at the object as if you had never seen an object of that sort before. Look at the colors, the shape, the design. Let your eyes feast upon it. Let yourself be in awe of this object which, like you, is of the earth.

Ponder

Hold the object before God, asking for openness to earth's messages. Now let the object "speak" to you. Does it suggest anything to you about yourself and your life? Let feelings and images come to you.

There are many messages you can hear in this way. A woman in one of my meditation classes once told me that, while she had always thought of her life as pointless, going around in circles like the grooves on a phonograph record, she realized as she gazed upon the delicate grooves of a clam shell ending in a single point that her life had meaning after all. That meaning was the "still point" in which all things converge—God.

Permit

As a result of your meditation, is there a way in which your life can reflect the harmony of earth's messages? For the woman with the clam shell, "permit" meant that she placed that shell on her desk to remind her of God's presence at the times when she became despondent.

To conclude, take a moment to offer a prayer of gratitude to God for this time of listening to earth's messages, before returning to the activities of daily life.

DREAMS

The pattern of prepare, picture, ponder, and permit is an excellent method of working with dreams, a form of communication with God that has roots both in scripture and Christian tradition.

Prepare

The major part of the preparation, of course, is remembering the dream. It helps to have a notebook near your bed, in which you can record your dreams as soon as you awaken. I remember, for example, a dream I had during the period that I was commuting almost daily to New York City to attend seminary. In my dream, I was sailing down a canal in a boat. As I neared the city, the canal became more and more shallow. Finally, my boat ran aground and I had to carry it to the far side of the city, where once again I found deep water.

Picture

Relax and breathe slowly as you try to enter your dream again imaginatively. What feelings does it evoke? What words come to mind? What are the recurring symbols? Does it remind you of other dreams you have had? In my "boat dream" I recognized two themes that frequently occur in my dreams: journeying and water. I remembered feeling frustrated and fatigued when my boat ran aground amidst the confusion of the city.

Ponder

Ask God to teach you through this dream. Bear in mind that the language of the dream is the language of *pictures* rather than words. What do the pictures in your dreams suggest? If you translated what they mean into words, what would they say to you? It was not difficult to discover what my dream was telling me: I needed the deep water of solitude and prayer in order to continue my life's journey, or my journey would be fatiguing and without any depth. It had been easy to ignore that need because of a heavy seminary schedule, but my dream would not allow me to ignore it. Sometimes the messages are not as obvious as this one was, however, and books on dream interpretation can be helpful in increasing your recognition of the vocabulary of your dreams.[1]

Permit

What will be the effect of the new self-awareness you have gained from this time of pondering your dream? After my dream, for example, I carved more time out of my daily activities for solitude and prayer. Since dreams generally tell us things about ourselves that we have not yet recognized in our conscious minds, praying our dreams can be a powerful source of transformation.

You may wish to close your prayer time with a prayer of gratitude for the gifts that sleep provides.

ART

We can also use the format of the four "P's" for meditating upon a work of visual art. One day, I stood before a Flemish Annunciation in the Metropolitan Museum of Art with a friend who was a curator. As we looked at the scene, where the angel Gabriel is pictured greeting a startled Mary, my friend explained the historical and artistic background of the work. I learned what the painter intended and the context in which he had painted. I soon found myself reflecting on what the painting meant to me.

I began to realize that both Mary and the Angel of the Annunciation could be understood as facets of my own personality. In this scene, Mary was drawing back in fear and wonder at the message of God's call to her. I recognized that a similar drama of reluctance and acceptance plays time and time again within my own heart. When I can reach the point of saying, "Let it be with me according to your word," I have accepted the angel's message, and a new life and liveliness are born. On the other hand, I am the angel, too. As a Christian, I have a responsibility for calling out new life in other people, playing—to put it rather dramatically—the role of a messenger from God. I could have pondered for hours, but then we moved on to another painting!

These have been just a few suggestions about the pattern of *prepare, picture, ponder, and permit,* but you may well think of further ways to use the pattern. Reflective prayer instills the habit of viewing *life itself* as a constant source of meditation. It helps us trust that, no matter what life brings, it can be illuminated by prayer. This is more than a pious exercise. It is potentially life-changing, since we open ourselves to the fullness of life intended by God, who created us as thinking, imaginative beings.

Breathing Space

1. Just as reflective prayer renews those unseen parts of us that Ignatius labeled "imagination, memory, intellect, and will," so the oxygen we breathe travels throughout the circulatory system, bringing new life to each part of the body and cleansing us of toxins. One way of becoming more aware of this reality is to take note of the movement of various parts of the body as we breathe.

Find a position in which you can rest completely, such as lying on your back with your knees bent and your feet on the floor, sitting in a chair with the back straight and supported, or even standing quietly. Close your eyes and focus your attention on different parts of the body in turn.

Take some time to notice how your abdomen moves as you inhale and exhale. Then picture the oxygen traveling down each leg into the feet. Now bring your attention to the floor of your pelvis, and notice how it broadens on each inhalation. Next, begin to notice how your sacrum (the large triangular bone that anchors the lower back into the pelvis) and the coccyx (or tailbone) move as you inhale and exhale. You will feel the lower part of your back, or lumbar spine, curving very gently as you breathe in and elongating as you breathe out. Continue by observing your entire spinal column. Picture your spine as a piece of driftwood, floating up and down on top of the wave of your breath.

Bring your awareness to your hipbones. If you press your hands against the side of your hips, you will feel how the swelling motion of your inhalation causes them to broaden slightly out of the hip sockets. Notice your rib cage. Can you feel the spaces between your ribs expanding on the inhalation and retracting on the exhalation?

Now, if you have been lying on your back, take a sitting or standing position. Bring your attention to your shoulders. As you inhale, see if you can feel the entire shoulder girdle broadening, from the breastbone through the collarbones to the shoulder sockets. You may even notice your arms rotating gently away from the center as you inhale and rotating inward as you exhale.

Next imagine your brain like a light bulb, glowing brightly on the inhalation and dimming on the exhalation. Feel the back of your skull expanding and broadening as you inhale and relaxing as you exhale.

Now, in any position you wish to take, imagine that your skin is like a stretchy "unitard," a one-piece dancer's leotard that covers the torso, legs, and arms. Visualize it stretching as you inhale, and retracting as you exhale.

❧

2. The previous exercise helped you to "send" your breath throughout the body. You can go a step further, sending your breath to specific areas of the body that need healing. Perhaps you have had a physical therapist who has massaged a muscle in spasm and suggested that you "breathe into" the pain. Or you have learned about or experienced natural childbirth, in which you surrender to the contractions by breathing into them, rather than resisting any discomfort they might cause.

You can use this technique to send healing energy to any part of your body. Take a moment to scan the body, noting where there is tension, discomfort, or even pain. Then relax and sit quietly, centering your attention upon the movement of the breath. Do you have a headache? Let the breath help to release the tension at the site of the pain. Indigestion? Exaggerate the expansion and contraction of the chest, abdomen, and ribcage as you breathe, sending calm breath to the digestive system. A muscle in spasm? The movement of the breath can help relax the muscle from the *inside,* similar to an external massage by healing hands.

The breath carries healing throughout the body, reminding us that the energy of God's Spirit constantly offers us the gift of wholeness.

In you God's energy is shown,
to us your varied gifts make known.
Teach us to speak, teach us to hear;
yours is the tongue and yours the ear.

HYMN 501, VERSE 3

Chapter Five

The Breath of God as Speech

Verbal Prayer

When we first meet someone, we use words in order to communicate. Our words are often requests. "I would like a round-trip ticket to New York City." "Would you please open the door?" Sometimes they are questions. "What is your name?" "Where do you come from?" As our friendships deepen, we articulate some of our deeper thoughts and feelings:

"I am sorry that I made you late." "I am angry because you did not keep your word." "I love you."

As we look back over our childhood memories, we can see that learning about God probably had its beginnings in the words we were taught to pray. "God bless Mommy and Daddy, and my cat, and please make Grandma well." "Now I lay me down to sleep, I pray the Lord my soul to keep." We continue to ask God for health and protection throughout life, but as we gain in intimacy with God our conversation includes much more: love, gratitude, penitence, anxiety, and even anger. The Psalms and the writings of the Hebrew prophets provide a good example of such prayer, as in Jeremiah's "Why is my pain unceasing?" (Jeremiah 15:18) and the psalmist's "I will give you thanks, O LORD, with my whole heart" (Psalm 138:1) and "Search me, O God, and know my heart" (Psalm 139:23).

People of the Judeo-Christian tradition are people of the word. In the Bible, we read of the power of the word to bless or to curse. A poet friend once read to me a poem she had written entitled "The Words Are Out," which dramatized the eternal vibrations and effects of the words we often speak unthinkingly. Words are powerful, for they express our thoughts. They are not just sounds or scribblings on a page. St. John the Evangelist calls Jesus himself God's Word or *Logos.*

Particularly since the invention of the printing press, to say nothing of radio, television, cell-phones, and e-mail, westerners have been bombarded with words. We learn speed-reading so that we can skim through literature, even the Bible. It is easy to forget the power of the spoken word. We tend to become so familiar with our liturgies that we may begin merely to mouth the words. It is even tempting to let personal verbal prayer become a mere repetition of formulae.

In a discussion of verbal or vocal prayer, therefore, the task is one of relearning how to *pray* words, rather than merely saying them, and to expand the scope of our prayer. To use the physiology of breath, it is somewhat like learning to breathe from the whole of the lungs rather than merely from the upper chest. Permitting the Creator's breath to breathe through our prayer means speaking about our whole experience of life, not just part of it. If we conceive of God as a distant figure, our prayer tends to be mostly petition, but if we understand God as closer to us than our very breath, our prayer can be honest conversation covering the entire spectrum of our life.

Such eminent teachers of prayer as the English author Evelyn Underhill and the retired Archbishop of Jerusalem George Appleton have made personal collections of prayers that had particular meaning for them, and we would do well to follow their examples.[1] There is a treasure trove of verbal prayer in the books of prayers intended for the public worship, such as *The Book of Common Prayer.* You may also wish to write your own prayers, as informal "letters to God" in your journal or as carefully crafted prose or poetry, and start your own notebook of prayers you collect.

There are many occasions for verbal prayer throughout the day as well as during your special prayer time. For some people, "praying without ceasing" takes the form of ongoing interior conversation with God—often in short prayers known as "arrow prayers." They can be a "Thank you, God," for receiving that long-awaited letter, or a short "Please protect him" as your son takes off in the family car. Even an automatic expression of dismay—"O my God!"—can be transformed into a prayer of trust that God is in the midst of every moment in our lives. Perhaps, in looking over your day's activities, you can discover certain times for habitual arrow prayers, such as a short prayer of penitence and renewal as you wash your face, or a prayer of praise as you awaken in the morning.

When we look at the place of words in the rhythm of silence, thought, word, and action that nurtures the breath of God in our lives, our best model is the prayer taught by Jesus himself, in response to the disciples' request: "Lord, teach us to pray." The Lord's Prayer illustrates the multiple facets of conversation with God. In the terminology of the Christian spiritual tradition, these facets are adoration, praise, thanksgiving, oblation, intercession, petition, and penitence. I have added the category of "trust."

Since this cherished prayer demonstrates the full spectrum of conversation with God, I will use it as an illustration of the ways we can breathe our verbal prayer more deeply. Along with the text of the prayer, I will reflect on each category as well as on the text itself. In addition, I will suggest ways you can make the bodyspirit connection, if you wish, by pointing out positions and movements that convey the meaning of the prayer. Experiment with the movements. Continue to use the ones you find helpful when you pray this prayer in private. Even when you do not use the movements, however, the memory of how they felt will transform your sense of the text. Even if you simply *imagine* your body doing the movements, they will help to deepen the prayer's meaning for you.

For our purposes, we will use the Lord's Prayer in its modern version—though of course it makes little difference which words you use. Both versions, after all, are translations from the original prayer, which was first taught in Aramaic and then recorded in the Greek of the gospels.

Our Father in heaven,
hallowed be your Name,
your kingdom come,

your will be done, on earth as in heaven.
Give us today our daily bread.
Forgive us our sins
as we forgive those who sin against us.
Save us from the time of trial,
and deliver us from evil.
For the kingdom, the power, and the glory are yours,
now and for ever. Amen.

OUR FATHER IN HEAVEN,
HALLOWED BE YOUR NAME

God-language is a sensitive issue today, since half the world's
population is excluded by traditional masculine imagery for
God. One way to deal with this sense of exclusion is to look
at what Jesus might have meant when he used the phrase
"Our Father." The first-century Aramaic word for father,
abba, conveyed the nurturing, loving quality of the relationship between a Jewish father and son. We can look beyond
the English word "father" to recognize God as a nurturing
parent, or even choose other ways of expressing the name of
God. The editors of *A New Zealand Prayer Book* offer some
alternatives, in their evocative translation of the Lord's
Prayer:

Eternal Spirit,
Earth-maker, Pain-bearer, Life-giver,
Source of all that is and that shall be,
Father and Mother of us all,
· Loving God, in whom is heaven.[2]

Choose an appropriate movement to express this saluta-
tion. First inhale and exhale, noticing the movement of the
breath. Then you may choose to inhale and reach with both
arms upward, like a toddler who wishes to be picked up by
her parent. Or you may reach down toward the earth and
then make a large circle with the arms to indicate the cosmos.
Or you may contract the abdominal muscles and fold the
head and the arms inward. Which of these movements
expresses your concept of *abba?*

Adoration

Heaven is wherever God's presence is known. For years, I
kept in one of my prayer books a small card that read, "All
the way to heaven is heaven, for he has said, 'I am the Way.'"
King Alfred said the same thing in different words: "Thou art
the journey and the journey's end." Begin your prayer by
acknowledging the heaven that is near to you, rather than a
heaven far off in time and space. Think of the wonder of
God's life moving through you with each breath. Think of the

vastness and wonder of creation, from the awesomeness of the night sky to the intricacies of a butterfly's wing. Begin your prayer with adoration: acknowledging God's holiness with a response of wonder, love, and awe. Adoration puts the rest of your prayer time into the proper perspective.

What is the natural way for your body to express adoration? Prostrating yourself on the ground, face downward? Standing and bending forward toward the earth? Lifting the arms to the sides, palms upward, in the ancient *orans* position of prayer? Other ways?

Praise

The natural sequence after adoration of God's holy presence is a prayer of praise, acknowledging not only your awe of God, but your joy as well. In human conversation, you would use the words, "You are wonderful!" Think of the times of your life when you have felt this joy. How did you react at those times? Perhaps you caught sight of a doe a few feet away in the woods, and you gasped with delight. Or you were so happy about the good fortune of a friend or family member that you wanted to dance and sing.

Explore ways to express praise in movement, perhaps postures that reach upward and give the body a light-hearted feeling, or rapid motions of hands and feet, like skipping or clapping, or even just letting the movement of your exhalations breathe forth "praise."

Thanksgiving

For what specific things do you give thanks to God? What blessings are a part of your life? Begin with the people who are important to you: spouse, children, parents, grandchildren, siblings, friends. Or the beauty of earth and sky. Good health or satisfying work. A cherished pet. A comfortable home. Sufficient food.

If your life seems devoid of blessings right now, the fact remains that God's love for you is so great that Jesus Christ shared in human loneliness, poverty, homelessness, and crucifixion, and you can thank God for that love. At particularly dark times, find consolation in your solidarity with God's other children around the world who are suffering. Difficult times in our lives can either isolate and embitter us or give us a greater understanding of our unity with the whole human family.

In conveying thankfulness through movement, the gesture of holding your blessings symbolically in the palms of the hands, stretched out in front of the chest, can be expressive. Or try moving your hands in the air as if you were creating a kind of "halo" around those things for which you are grateful.

YOUR KINGDOM COME,
YOUR WILL BE DONE,
ON EARTH AS IN HEAVEN

Oblation

Oblation is the offering of oneself for the working out of God's purposes. It is the willingness to be the channel of the breath of God in the world.

To offer ourselves, we need to accept ourselves. If each of us is a unique creation of God, our oblation is an offering of *our* uniqueness, not of someone else's. God imagines more for you than you can begin to imagine. Honor God's imagination. Dare to offer God your potential self, as well as your present self, and be willing to take practical steps in order to grow more and more in accord with God's imagination for you. You are meant to become part of the "kingdom-come" process, helping to work out God's purposes through sharing the breath of God.

What gestures or movement convey offering? You will probably wish to find a movement of openness, with the palms up, ready to give as well as to receive. You may wish to make this gesture in all directions, as well as upward and downward. Or you may wish to explore the kinds of gestures that portray your particular ways of helping God's kingdom to come on earth as it is in heaven.

GIVE US TODAY OUR DAILY BREAD

Petition

Petition is "asking prayer." Since God is our nurturing parent, our prayer includes confiding our needs to God. Although God knows our needs better than we ourselves know them, part of our companionship with God is learning the humility to share those needs, no matter how trivial they may seem to us. We need hold nothing back through false pride or piety. Humility has as its root the word *humus*—earth! Remember that you are an earthling, in need of bread as well as of many other things, both earthly and heavenly.

Intercession

Intercession is "asking prayer" on behalf of others. The thought of this may be overwhelming: how can one possibly pray for all the needs of a broken world? In answering this question, I offer the example provided by the Society of Friends. It is through their practice of sitting in silence that Quakers discover, individually and also as a community, what their specific "concerns" are. They feel that God calls them to address, through prayer and through action, the specific concerns that come to light. When we feel overwhelmed by the needs of the entire world, it is helpful to try to discover our *specific* concerns.

Find an inner stillness before you pray. As you sit quietly, the thought of another person may come to your mind, sometimes even with a sense of urgency that might be interpreted as an inner demand to pray for that person. Another way to discover your special concerns is to read the newspaper, and to hold before God those situations that most capture your attention. You may also wish to build up a personal list of people for whom you will pray regularly during your intercessions.

Intercession is an expression of the reality of the communion of saints, and is a way of expressing our unity with others, both in this life and beyond the grave. All things in this world are connected; the ill-health or ill-fortune of one member of the human race affects us all. We are children of the same Creator. We breathe the same air. There is no A-positive or B-negative breath. Moreover, we are discovering that the ill-health or ill-fortune of other species of the creation of God affect humanity as well. We are dependent upon the health of the whole earth. I remember being awe-struck when I learned in elementary school that the oxygen we breathe has been exhaled by the plant life which, in turn, finds life in the carbon dioxide we exhale.

Prayers of petition and intercession are built on the foundation of our faith in God's closeness to us. Some understandings of these prayers are based on a concept of a distant

God who needs to be coaxed into helping us and those we love; from this perspective, the "success" of petition and intercession depends on how hard we pray and how "good" we are. If we have enough "faith," our prayers will be "answered." We need, however, to move past a Newtonian cause-and-effect universe, both in science and in spirituality. In holding our needs and those of others before God, we do so with an awareness of the connectedness of all things, and we contribute, through our prayer, to a mysterious and complex network of energy. It is not that we change the divine mind through our prayer. Rather, we help "God's will be done" through our prayer. Archbishop William Temple once said, "When I pray, coincidences happen. When I stop praying, they cease."

This does not mean that our needs as we perceive them are necessarily met. The freedom that God bequeathed upon the universe at its creation has resulted in what clearly seems like random evil, and the human capacity for egocentricity and violence cannot easily be changed. We are told by Jesus Christ to pray for our needs, nevertheless. For we are called to be, through our prayer and our action, co-creators and channels of God's love, which, as the poet Dante points out, "moves the sun and the other stars" as well as our own world.

In seeking a gesture to express petition and intercession, I inevitably find myself cupping my hands and holding them out in front of me. They represent both my expectation of receiving God's care and love, and my offering of the needs about which I pray. Sometimes I hold in my palms a mental picture of the people or situation, like a hologram held before God.

Another way to embody these prayers is actually to express your specific concerns through the vocabulary of movement. I have led workshops in which, for example, we have each danced those parts of the environment we prayed for: some people made the wave-like motions of the ocean, some stretched tall like the trees of the rainforests, while some "became" an endangered species. It is a powerful experience to put oneself in the shoes—or lack thereof—of the homeless person on the street: to feel the weakness of the body, the hardness of the sidewalk on which one sleeps, the gnawing hunger in the belly, or the disorientation of the mind. Or to imagine oneself as a child in a war-torn city: to feel the rapid heartbeat of fear, to move like a frightened small animal against the crackling backdrop of gunfire.

FORGIVE US OUR SINS, AS WE FORGIVE THOSE WHO SIN AGAINST US

Penitence

Penitence means sorrow for sin. To be sorrowful for sin, one must first recognize sin. This involves what the Christian tradition calls "self-examination," or identifying our sins. One way of going about that task is to ask the question, "What impedes God's breath moving through me?"

When I was an adolescent, I used some self-examination questions contained in a small devotional book written in an earlier era. Some of these questions were about actions that broke "rules," and I have to admit that, in my naiveté, I sometimes had no idea what they were suggesting! Sometimes, on the other hand, the questions were about feelings, like anger or envy, that I could not help having, especially as a teenager. Overall, if my memory is correct, the questionnaire was somewhat lacking both in a healthy attitude about human emotions and in an understanding of sin's source in the human psyche.

I prefer now to look at sin as the ways we distort our humanity: How do we think and act in ways that deny our identity as "God-filled dust"? What obstacles are crowding the space that is meant to be holy space? I often tell the story of an actor friend who teaches voice production. He tells me that the most difficult part of the teaching process is to persuade people to exhale completely: "They want to keep just a little bit of the air in there, *just in case....* "

We all have thought patterns and behaviors we hold on to, "just in case," that need to be exhaled. We may have become comfortable with them, but at the very least they can prevent our fullness of life in God and at the worst they can suffocate us. Maybe the "just in case" takes the form of self-indulgence or self-centeredness or self-hatred. Maybe the "just in case" lurking in a dark corner of our psyche takes the ugly shape of hatred, prejudice, or blindness to the sufferings of others. Maybe it is greed or addiction that suffocates us. Maybe we just *partly* breathe because of laziness, complacency, or fear.

There are many guides to help us in identifying these thought patterns and behaviors. The Beatitudes and the Ten Commandments, especially if we look beyond the commandments to the picture of human wholeness that is their source, are age-old guidelines to righteous living. The Litany of Penitence in the Ash Wednesday liturgy in the Episcopal Church's *Book of Common Prayer* is a fine contemporary articulation of human sinfulness, and many other prayer books contain similar litanies. Among the writers of the Christian spiritual tradition, I find great wisdom in the insights of the poet Dante, who in the *Purgatorio* classifies all sin as disordered love—the ways we love too little, or too much, or love the wrong things—and who vividly portrays the effects of these distortions on the human self and the human community. While *all* prayer is, in the end, prayed in the context of community, the prayer of penitence, like intercession, is a specifically social prayer in its capacity to heal: it has the power to bring healing to ourselves and to our connection with the earth community in which we live.

In the prayer of penitence we become willing to exhale our sin in confession, in order to inhale the breath of healing and forgiveness. Just as the Genesis creation story helped us to understand our identity as "God-filled dust," a post-resurrection story from the gospel of John can serve as a dramatization of the healing and forgiveness that is also the gift of God:

> When it was evening on that day, the first day of the week, and the doors of the house where the disciples had met were locked for fear of the Jews, Jesus came and stood among them and said, "Peace be with you." After he said this, he showed them his hands and his side. Then the disciples rejoiced when they saw the Lord. Jesus said to them again, "Peace be with you. As the Father has sent me, so I send you." When he had said this, he breathed on them and said to them, "Receive the Holy Spirit. If you forgive the sins of any, they are forgiven them; if you retain the sins of any, they are retained." (John 20:19-23)

While this story tells us that Jesus gave his disciples the power to forgive sins, it assures us all of the power of God's forgiveness as we confess our sins to God, whether in personal prayer or in the presence of another person.

Do you recognize the elements of that story? The internal breezes were stormy ones. The disciples were afraid, as were the members of John's community of Christian Jews who were in conflict with the non-Christian Jews of the synagogue at the time of the writing of this gospel. ("For fear of the Jews" must be understood in this historical context, because the disciples in question were also, of course, Jews.) And Jesus came and said, "Peace." With that peace came a calming of the storm, a healing of terror. Jesus' breath brought not only the healing of the disciples' fear, but the power to heal the physical and spiritual wounds of others, as well. We, like the disciples, can become healthy and life-giving by breathing in the loving power of God and letting that power transform our inner environment.

As we ourselves become healed and forgiven, we can let ourselves receive another gift: the gift of giving what we have received—the power to forgive others the wrongs they have done us. It might even have been better to put it this way: "Forgive us our sins, *so that* we can forgive those who sin against us."

As you explore the ways you can use movement to express healing and forgiveness, think of this part of the prayer as a process: from muscular tension to relaxation, from a closed posture to an open one, from a heavy bowed stance to a light and uplifted one, or from a position in which you are cut off from others to one in which you connect with others. You may better understand some of your specific areas of sinfulness through improvising the way they feel to you. For example, if you have discovered anger that is destructive of another person or yourself, dance as if you are angry. You will notice the incredible amount of energy that anger produces. Keep dancing, and explore ways to use that energy, perhaps through hard physical effort doing something that you enjoy, or in using the energy creatively to change the situation causing your anger.

Last but not least, remember the power for healing of the movement of the breath. The most healing thing we can do, in the end, is to breathe great draughts of God's love, our free gift from our Creator, and the movement of our physical breath helps us to do that. Remember that the catalyst for much of our sinfulness is, paradoxically, the emptiness that is a sign of our desire for God. Notice the emptiness as you exhale, and then notice the lungs filling. Begin to move with the inhalations and exhalations, noticing the freedom that moving with an acceptance of the rhythm of the breath can bring.

SAVE US FROM THE TIME OF TRIAL,
AND DELIVER US FROM EVIL.
FOR THE KINGDOM, THE POWER, AND

THE GLORY ARE YOURS,
NOW AND FOR EVER. AMEN.

Trust

In the prayer of trust, we ask God's empowerment in living
our Christian faith and we place all our anxieties in God's
hands. Although we would prefer not to be subjected to times
of trial or of evil, we have the assurance that God will be with
us during those times of suffering that are an inevitable part
of life, as well as during the times when we experience the
"kingdom, the power, and the glory." Two passages of scripture that illustrate this prayer are the beloved twenty-third
psalm, "Though I walk through the valley of the shadow of
death, I shall fear no evil; for you are with me; your rod and
your staff, they comfort me" (23:4 BCP), and the passage in
the book of Job where God's voice answers Job out of the
whirlwind: "Where were you when I laid the foundation of
the earth?" (38:4). With God's presence in all things, from the
beginning of time, there is nothing ultimately to fear, in life or
in death. You might think of this prayer as a deep relaxed
breath, or sigh of relief.

How would you express this prayer in movement? I sup-
pose that permitting your body to relax completely is one
way. Another way is to make an offering gesture once again,
with the arms raised in front of the chest, palms upward.
"The kingdom, the power, and the glory" can be expressed by

reaching and stretching, with particular energy given to the word "power," or by a profound bow—whichever seems most natural to you. "Amen" may be expressed by assuming a prayer posture with the hands—either palms together, palms upward, or hands raised to the sides in the *orans* position.

We have spent an extended time with the Lord's Prayer, for it illustrates a way to offer our words to God "with the whole capacity of the lungs." As part of the repertoire of prayer, verbal prayer will always be a part of the speech of the worshiping Christian. Whether we use this beloved prayer from the Christian tradition, the words in our prayer books, or our own words, there is nothing we need hide from the One who knows us better than we know ourselves.

Breathing Space

The human brain is not merely a mass of undifferentiated gray matter. Rather—to vastly oversimplify—it consists of two hemispheres, right and left, connected by a bundle of nerves called the *corpus callosum*. The brain is a miracle of complexity and balance. Each hemisphere has its tasks. The right is the domain of creativity—poetry, puns, holistic and concrete thought—and of dreams, what we might call the "unconscious." The left hemisphere is the domain of words and logic—of linear, literal, and abstract thought. Scientists tell us that the experience of the right hemisphere travels across the *corpus callosum* in order to be expressed verbally. You may have had an experience similar to what happened to me in seminary, when I went from a class on spirituality and contemplative prayer to a class on church history and found it difficult to switch mental gears from the right hemisphere to the left. It always took me several minutes to settle down and take notes, because of the adjustment in the way I was required to *think*.

My adjustment from a class on spirituality to a class on church history mirrors what some theologians tell us about religious experience. Our primary experience of Holy Mystery has its source, most likely, in the right hemisphere. But it remains unarticulated until somehow the experience journeys across the *corpus callosum* into the left hemisphere so that we are able to express it, think about it, and grow from it.

Alternate nostril breathing is an ancient eastern exercise that at first might seem quite exotic. However, it not only helps us physiologically: it also mirrors the importance of our contemporary knowledge about brain function. When we practice it, we "send oxygen" (whether it is real oxygen or "psychological oxygen" matters little) to both hemispheres of the brain equally, creating a state of harmony and balance.

Sit on a chair. Place the index and middle fingers of your right hand on the bridge of your nose, letting the thumb rest lightly beside the right nostril and the ring finger beside the left nostril. (It is a good idea to alternate hands, either using the right hand one day and the left the next, or each day performing half of the exercise with each hand.) Bow your head slightly downward, but keep your upper torso erect. Try not to let your head be pulled off-center by your hand.

There are two ways to perform this exercise.

1. With your thumb, close the right nostril, breathing in through the left nostril only. Then release the right nostril and breathe out through both nostrils.

Then close the left nostril with the ring finger, breathing in through the right nostril only. Release and breathe out through both nostrils.

Continue this pattern up to twenty cycles, counting up to 4, 5, or 6 on each inhalation and exhalation, according to the rhythm that is most comfortable for you.

2. Close the left nostril and exhale completely through the right nostril. With your thumb, close the right nostril, breathing in through the left nostril only.

Then close the left nostril and exhale through the right nostril. Then inhale through the right nostril, close the right nostril, and exhale through the left nostril.

Continue alternating nostrils, first exhaling and then inhaling with each nostril in turn. Count up to 4, 5, or 6 on each inhalation and exhalation, according to the rhythm that is most comfortable for you.

Practicing this exercise is an excellent way to balance the body and mind and to calm the nerves. I like to see it as a symbol of our ability to "think" from both hemispheres of the brain. Breathing the *ruach* of God both into our unconscious experience of the divine and into our communication of that experience helps draw us to new unity, in which our senses are awakened, our courage is bolstered, and our love is kindled.

Flood our dull senses with your light;
in mutual love our hearts unite.
Your power the whole creation fills;
confirm our weak, uncertain wills.

HYMN 501, VERSE 4

Chapter Six

The Breath of God as Action

We have explored in the three previous chapters how we grow in intimacy with God through silence, thought, and speech. This chapter adds to those traditional ways of praying the category of prayer as action.

How does prayer as the breath of God express itself in action? I think that, first of all, we need to understand the connection between the "inhalation" we usually call prayer and the "exhalation" called action. If prayer is true prayer, it takes us not *out* of the world but *into* the midst of the world's concerns. We might think of prayer as following a spiral into the very center of ourselves. One would expect that the center would be small, but it is just the opposite. This spiral is in three, or perhaps four, dimensions: the center of the spiral is a break-through into the vastness of God—the God who holds the whole creation in being, from the sun and the moon and the rain forest to the "itty bitty baby," in the words of the spiritual. So it is not surprising that we meet, right at the still center of things, the urgency of the world's needs.

The spiral's center is like the wardrobe door in C. S. Lewis's *The Lion, the Witch, and the Wardrobe* that opens into the vast new world called Narnia, which is more "real" than the real world. It is like Alice falling down a narrow rabbit hole into the wide world of Wonderland. It is like dipping ever more deeply into a well until you reach groundwater.

The spiraling inward journey of prayer is a journey in which we bring with us the whole of life. We need leave nothing behind. My husband and I used to prepare a gigantic "spider web" in the basement for our sons' birthday parties. We constructed the web by crisscrossing lengths of twine attached to a clothespin bearing a small guest's name; at the end of the twine was a hidden party favor. At the signal "go," each child would begin winding up the string around the clothespin. Imagine the merriment, and sometimes the frustration, of the game—and how like life it is! As we travel along life's journey to God, we wind into our prayer all that we have been and all that we have done, and throughout we are connected to God, "the journey and the journey's end."

The journey inward takes us to infinite horizons where we experience the world in the light of the Trinity, whose chief characteristic is interrelationship and communication. Christian prayer can never be the "flight of the alone to the Alone," because even God is not alone. The love that radiates among the persons of the Trinity suggests that we cannot keep God's breath to ourselves, any more than we can survive in a physical sense by holding our breath. We need to communicate our prayer: to exhale as well as inhale.

It is in sharing the breath and life of God that we become agents of transformation in our world. The Orthodox tradition speaks of *synergeia*—synergy, or cooperation with God. If we cooperate with God through using the energy and insight we have received in prayer, our prayer becomes action, and that action, in turn, becomes a form of prayer. The Hindu spiritual leader Mohandas Gandhi expressed the concept well: "The task of the true servant of society...is to prepare in interior silence and consecrated action a place for the future to be born."

Prayer as action can take many forms. Think of the many ways we reveal ourselves through what we do: the ethical choices we make, our artistic creativity, the way we go about our daily work, the way we treat our family and friends, the way we hold our bodies, the tone of our voice, the quality of our gestures.

As prayer becomes more and more a part of your life, you will probably be drawn to consider the ways in which you express your faith in terms of lifestyle or ethical choices. Your sense of a righteous and loving God will make it no longer possible to pass the bag lady on the street without at least a pang, to enjoy the harboring of personal resentments, or to cheat blithely on your income tax. A subtle transformation begins to take place.

Working for social justice and peace is an obvious form of prayer as action, of exhaling the power that God has breathed into us on behalf of others. Mother Teresa of Calcutta began each day with a period of meditation that was the source of her energy to serve the poor. The statesman Dag Hammarskjöld left us in his diary *Markings* a moving document of an ongoing interior dialogue with God. Gandhi saw the future of the world born out of the womb of interior silence. You may have glimpsed this truth in your own prayer. Perhaps, as you have prayed, some concern outside yourself seems to have intruded, along with a sense that you should perform some action.

We have already mentioned the tradition in the Society of Friends of communal centering leading to a discernment of social concerns. It is in the rhythm of inhalation and exhalation that the social involvement so typical of Quakers has its source, and followers of that way have been among the first to protest some of society's horrors, from slavery to war.

It is important to remember the inward source of our action, for without it social activism can become rootless and breathless. Gandhi's advice to "prepare in interior silence" is well taken, so that our action can indeed become a breathing forth of God's power. If we remember that our action has its source in God, we can perhaps avoid our propensities to control others through our service to them. If we can remember that it is God's breath—not our own—that we breathe forth in our service, we may even avoid the burnout caused by using our useful action as a means of bolstering our sense of self-esteem.

Some people are called to express the breath of God through creative work rather than through overt social action. The most obvious case is the artist, who communicates God's vibrant life through the language of music, dance, poetry, architecture, painting, or sculpture. The expression of inner reality through the concrete outer forms of the arts is a familiar pattern for these pioneers of the spirit, from the builders of medieval cathedrals to the artists of today who employ all their skill in the act of creation for the glory of God. I think of Isadora Duncan, who wrote that she spent "long days and nights in the studio seeking that dance which might be a divine expression of the human spirit through the body's movement," and her compatriot, the Parisian organist, composer, and mystic Olivier Messiaen, whose music communicates to many people the mystery of God.

It should not be surprising that the artistic enterprise finds its source at the center of the spiral where our life touches God, the Creator. Deep prayer opens up the unconscious mind, where great creative potential is stored. "Inspiration" has its root, after all, in the word *spiritus*—breath, or spirit. I once taught a meditation class in tandem with a teacher of creative writing who followed my session with a session of poetry writing. She was amazed to discover how easily the poetry flowed from her students when it was composed by minds that were relaxed and meditative. You also may have found that the quiet of prayer is conducive to creative ideas. Some teachers of prayer label those ideas "distractions" and tell students to ignore them. My own preference is to keep paper and pen handy in order to record the ideas I do not wish to lose; then I can let the ideas go until prayer time is over.

It is not merely the activist's or artist's vocation that can become prayer as action, but *all* work, from preparing a meal to serving on a school committee. In an essay by Dorothy Sayers entitled *Why Work?*, the author counsels that we should look on all work not as a necessary drudgery to be undergone for the purpose of making money, but as a way of life in which the nature of man should find its proper exercise and delight and so fulfil itself to the glory of God. That it should, in fact, be thought of as a creative activity undertaken for the love of the work itself; and that man, made in God's image, should make things, as God makes them, for the sake of doing well a thing that is well worth doing.[1]

The tasks of each day, as well as the times of rest and recreation, are all part of the raw material—the *adamah*—of our prayer, rather than things we must finish in order to spend time in "real prayer." If we can grasp the truth that no moment of our lives will ever come again, we will begin to value every breath and learn to move through our days with what Buddhists call "mindfulness." To be mindful means to focus our attention fully on what we are doing. The fourteenth-century German mystic Meister Eckhart expressed it well: "Wisdom consists in doing the next thing you have to do, doing it with your whole heart, and finding delight in doing it."

Breathing forth our prayer as action implies that we take responsibility as earthlings, for we are citizens of the earth

that is home for all of us. The earth itself, writes the biologist
Lewis Thomas, breathes:

> When the earth came alive it began by constructing its
> own membrane, for the general purpose of editing the
> sun.... The earth breathes, in a certain sense.... It is
> hard to feel affection for something as totally imper-
> sonal as the atmosphere, and yet there it is, as much a
> part and product of life as wine or bread. Taken all in
> all, the sky is a miraculous achievement. It works, and
> for what it is designed to accomplish it is as infallible
> as anything in nature. I doubt whether any of us could
> think of a way to improve on it, beyond maybe shift-
> ing a local cloud from here to there on occasion. The
> word "chance" does not serve to account well for
> structures of such magnificence.[2]

The word "chance" does not serve well, for the breathing
of the atmosphere, like our own respiration, is the creation of
God, and it is incumbent upon us to respect the earth's life-
breath as if it were our own, which indeed it is. We need to
continue to breathe life into all the aspects of human community through our action, and to breathe forth God in
words, music, dance, art, science, and in all the work we
undertake. We need to breathe forth truth as we each understand it. Finally, standing awe-struck before the magnificence

of life, we need to breathe forth praise, and worship with our actions the goodness of the Creator.

Breathing Space

Stand, feeling the weight of your body descending through your legs and feet into the earth, as if your feet could grow roots into the ground. Note the upward stretch of the body as you inhale. Our bodies express both our reaching toward the One who fills us with life and our rootedness in the earth that, for now, is the home given us by our Creator. We live within these two realities, which, like the rhythm of our breath, is not a static state but a dynamic one. Both for our body's health and our spirit's well-being, we are healthiest if we stretch, reach, and move. Some simple stretching exercises which help us open our lungs can remind us of this.

1. Stand (or sit on a stool) with your arms hanging at your sides, then reach behind your back with your arms straight, interlocking your fingers, if possible. Imagine that someone is pulling your hands downward toward the floor. As you

inhale, lift and open the chest; as you exhale, let the arms drop down again to the sides. Repeat three times, directing your breath into the front of the chest.

2. Standing or seated, clasp your elbows with the opposite hands, and let your arms hang down in front of you, rounding your back and shoulders and dropping your head so that your body curls forward as you inhale. Feel the back of the ribcage expanding. Remain in that position as you exhale and inhale several more times, directing the breath into the back. Imagine that the back of your ribcage is like a bellows, opening and closing.

3. Standing or seated, stretch the right arm upward over the head and lean to the left as you inhale. "Breathe into" the right side of the ribcage, as if it were a bellows, opening and closing. Exhale as you come back to an upright position and drop the right arm.

Now do the exercise to the opposite side, stretching the left arm over the head toward the right, so that the left side of the ribcage can expand and contract as you breathe.

Stretching and moving with our bodies prepares our hearts and spirits so that we can move outside our narrow self-interest when we hear God's call to help bring peace and healing to a world in sore need. When we are confronted with danger, fear, and uncertainty, it is tempting to curl up like an infant in an attitude of self-protection, at least metaphorically. Such a response brings no health either to ourselves or to the world around us. Instead, we can breathe the *ruach* of God and, in the words of the old hymn, "stretch every nerve and press with vigor on" as citizens of earth and of God's kingdom.

From inner strife grant us release;
turn nations to the ways of peace.
To fuller life your people bring
that as one body we may sing:

Praise to the Father, Christ, his Word,
and to the Spirit: God the Lord,
to whom all honor, glory be
both now and for eternity.

HYMN 501, VERSES 5, 6

Chapter Seven

The Breath of Life

We have now looked at prayer as silence, thought, speech, and action. The truth is, though, that while we can systematize ways of praying for the sake of convenience, all prayer is part of a single continuum. Since relationship with God is intertwined with all the complexity and variety of human experience, various approaches to prayer are like points on a circle. The four ways we have discussed might be compared to the poet John Donne's image of the "round earth's imagin'd corners."

Over the years in which I have taught about prayer, I have come to recognize that each person tends to be drawn to certain ways of praying. This may be due to the "imagin'd corners" of human temperament. The personality typology proposed by Isabel Myers and Katharine C. Briggs, based on the theories of the psychologist Carl Jung, is one way of expressing this variety of temperament. To vastly oversimplify a complex scheme, Myers and Briggs believed that each person relates to the world primarily through the senses, the intellect, the intuition, or the emotions. Their goal was to help people bring all of the functions into a balanced integration, since all four components are necessary in functioning as a whole human being.

The same can be said for our prayer. We limit ourselves and our prayer if we use only the mode of prayer that we happen to find most natural. Early in this century, the theologian and spiritual director Friedrich von Hügel described three "elements" of religion: the historical or institutional, the intellectual, and the mystical. He suggested that most people have an *attrait* or attraction to a particular element, but that religious growth tends to be marked by movement along a continuum that eventually results in an integration of all three. Among the people he counseled was the great teacher of prayer and scholar of mysticism Evelyn Underhill, whose natural prayer was contemplation. He advised her not to neglect the historical and institutional aspects of faith: she should find a community where she could worship regularly. Nor should she neglect the intellect: she should study the Bible and theology, but also secular subjects, because study trains the mind and broadens one's understanding of God's creation. Finally, he insisted that she involve herself in serving the dispossessed by becoming friends with a family in the slums of London. Although he did not label it as such, I would identify this activity as a fourth element, the "pastoral" element of religion.

You have probably already made the connection between the Myers-Briggs foursome and von Hügel's historical/institutional, intellectual, mystical—along with my own addition of pastoral. You may even be thinking about people you know who typify each *attrait,* bearing in mind that even these examples are "imagin'd corners," because both our personalities and our prayers defy easy categorization. To vastly oversimplify, the predominantly sensing person may find most fulfillment in the language of the institutional church, like the scholars who do the painstaking work of providing its liturgical resources, or the masters-of-ceremonies who ensure that corporate worship flows smoothly. The predominantly thinking person may find that reflection is the most natural way to God, like a theology professor I had in seminary whose faith came alive as he discussed the doctrines of Christianity. The intuitive person is likely to seek solitude for the prayer of contemplation; this is the natural prayer of many monastics and of a surprising number of people in the secular world, although they may not yet have recognized it. The person with a strong "feeling" capacity may wish to express relationship with God through service to others, by being, for example, the friend who is always eager and willing to help in a crisis.

Both Carl Jung and Friedrich von Hügel teach us to gain familiarity with the sides of our temperaments that may be least attractive to us. In this way, we become more integrated human beings and also can learn to appreciate people who function differently from us. Wholeness and holiness, to say nothing of compassion for others who are different, are found not in remaining stuck in one of the "imagin'd corners" but in exploring for oneself the full circle.

THE WEATHERS OF PRAYER

Another reason we need to become familiar with a variety of ways to pray is that different modes of prayer are helpful at different times of our lives, especially when we find it difficult to pray. The breath of God in us is not isolated from the atmosphere in which we live, any more than the homes in which we dwell are isolated from the weather outside. While a house does protect us, we still notice the shudders caused by a hurricane and the sultry heat in the kitchen during the hottest days of summer. There are times when our psychological "weather" affects our prayer, and flexibility can help us at those times. Just as the sky above us is not always blue nor is the breeze always gentle, so our interior weather can affect our prayer, even causing us to resist it, either consciously or unconsciously. A telltale symptom is that we put everything else first, and then complain that we have no time to pray!

Sometimes the interior weather is like the "doldrums," the mass of unmoving air found near the equator. Medieval spiritual guides called the doldrums *accidie,* or listlessness. When you are in the doldrums, prayer seems humdrum, since it is difficult to feel enthusiastic about anything. At a time like this, in particular, it will help to pray in a new and different way. For example, if you generally pray in a simple contemplative mode, try using a devotional book, or even write your prayers in a journal. If you are accustomed to praying with words, light a candle and silently focus on the flame, the symbol of God's light.

Or the breezes that blow may feel more like a duststorm. On windy days in both city and country, airborne debris—dust, leaves, gum-wrappers—can swirl in the air and blind the vision momentarily. The debris of your life can clutter your mind so that you cannot focus on prayer. If so, it may be necessary to sweep the air clear by spending extra time in preparation for prayer. Experiment with a yoga class or a long walk to shed physical tension. Find an activity that centers you, from arranging a bouquet of flowers to whittling some wood, in order to shed psychological tension. These preparations for prayer can themselves become a form of prayer, and in particularly chaotic times they may be all you can manage.

Or you may find yourself in gusty weather. I remember watching our two sons attempting to sail a small boat on a very small lake in upper New York State. Every time they would gather some speed in one direction, the wind would change. If you have ever been in a situation like this, you know what it is like to have too many directions in which you travel during prayer time. You may have agendas pulling you first in one direction, then another. You hope to come to some decision about a career change, to prepare a lecture or presentation, and at the same time clear the mind and focus on God's presence. If you come to prayer in gusty weather, try to shed the multiple goals and focus on only one for the duration of your time of prayer.

Have you ever experienced the overwhelming power of a hurricane? Hurricanes are much like the negative emotions that sometimes seem to overwhelm the spirit. As soon as you begin to pray, anger or depression may "blow you away," so that your attention is captivated by the emotion rather than centered on the presence of God. If you are in the midst of a hurricane, spend some extra time in releasing your physical tension. You may even need to incorporate some exercise like a vigorous walk or a swim into your pattern of prayer. As you exercise, let yourself transform the emotion into pure physical energy, like converting gasoline into motion. Another way to deal with emotional stormy weather is to rise above it as if you were in a weather plane, by engaging the mind fully in some study that becomes reflective prayer. There is nothing like a change of mental functioning to give us perspective on what seems, when we are in the midst of it, like an overpowering storm.

Perhaps your inner environment feels as if you are in the ominous presence of a tornado. I have been told that the pressure of a tornado can create such a vacuum inside a building that the building can explode unless the windows are opened. Are there windows in your spirit that need to be opened? Is the pressure of resentment, falsity, guilt, or inconsistency building up? The psychologist Roy Menninger, in an article entitled "Responsibility to Self," states that in our use of time and energy there are serious imbalances "within the life space of each of us," caused by the fact that our actual lives often do not reflect our beliefs.

> In spite of public protestations about the importance of the family, about the needs of the community, about the troubles in our world, most of us devote the smallest proportion of our time to these areas. . . . It is this

inconsistency which produces a subtle but corrosive tension as your conscience cries out for one commitment while your activities express another.[1]

Whatever causes our inward sense of pressure, we need to identify it and to free ourselves by confessing it, rather than letting it remain unexamined and repressed. The prayer of penitence may be the prayer that can clear the air.

Such alien breezes as the ones I have mentioned above can make it difficult indeed to begin to pray. Other resistance is caused by an unrecognized fear of prayer. We sense that we are venturing into uncharted territory. As we become silent and relaxed, we may be surprised by old memories we thought we had forgotten and fears we did not know we had. When we stop ruffling the water on the surface of a lake, it becomes calm and clear: the eye can finally perceive not only the beautiful fish and grasses on the bottom, but also some less attractive denizens of the deep, who may disgust or startle us. How do we deal with these negative things that come into view during our prayer?

It is trust in a loving God, as well as trust in the goodness of our creation as *adam,* God-filled dust, that can dispel our fear of prayer. With this foundation of faith, it is safe to shed our psychological fears as well as our physical tensions. In one of the post-resurrection appearances in John's gospel, it is the presence and breath of Jesus that dissolves the fear of the frightened disciples: "'Peace be with you. . . .' When he had said this, he breathed on them" (20:21-22). Let God's breath dissolve your fear and release your natural capacity to pray.

For prayer is as natural as breathing. This may sound obvious, but many of us have been taught to believe that we *ought* to pray because of the expectations of the church, because of some standard of "goodness," or because God will be offended if we do not pray. If you understand that you pray because it is your *nature* to pray, the whole dynamic of avoidance seems to change. For example, I used to think that if I missed a day or two in my "rule" of prayer, I somehow had to make it up, like homework or piano practice. That simply is not necessary! God understands us better than we understand ourselves. God understands the reasons we might not have prayed—whether for days, or weeks, or years. God is ready to have us begin right where we are. To accept that fact is a great source of freedom. Prayer is not our duty; rather, like inhalation, it is our life.

RHYTHM OF LIFE

Establishing a pattern in our prayer nurtures us as whole human beings. I call that pattern a "rhythm of life" rather than the more traditional "rule of life," because it better expresses the naturalness and freedom of the breath metaphor.

One way to create a structure for your rhythm of life is to make sure you have time and space to breathe the oxygen of the four "elements" of religion: institutional, intellectual, mystical, and pastoral.

The Institutional

In worship with others we are reminded that we are making life's journey not as solitary travelers, but in the company of Christians past and present. It is often tempting for people on a profound spiritual journey to cut their moorings from community, but experience has demonstrated that this kind of individualism produces rootlessness and restlessness.

Seek in humility the worshiping community with which you feel an affinity. There are many ways to worship with others, from small gatherings for silent prayer to liturgical worship that, at its best, integrates all the varieties of prayer we have discussed in this book.

The Intellectual

Engage your mind in study: the study of scripture first and foremost, but also of the classics of spirituality. Joseph Campbell writes:

> One of our problems today is that we are not well acquainted with the literature of the spirit.... When you get to be older, and the concerns of the day have all been attended to, and you turn to the inner life— well, if you don't know where it is or what it is, you'll be sorry.[2]

He includes in that literary category not only the sacred scriptures and mythologies of various traditions, but novels— "great novels." Von Hügel would have added the sciences, and I would add the arts, for delving into the creative processes and structures of these non-verbal languages of humankind is surely not only bracing intellectually but is itself a window opened toward the Creator.

The Mystical

It may surprise you to learn that this entire volume has been about the mystical element of religion. I believe that mysticism, rather than being an unusual form of religious experience known by a few people (mostly now deceased!), is everyone's basic way of knowing God. Mysticism simply means our *own* experience of God, not experience that we are given secondhand. I would hope that this book, in expanding the traditional definition of prayer to *all* the ways you relate to God in word, thought, silence, or action, has demonstrated that the mystical way is as natural as breathing, and is also the way to become fully human.

The Pastoral

Serve others by reaching out in whatever ways are appropriate for *you*. Do not feel that you need to copy anyone else. I remember filling out a questionnaire once on the "gifts of the Spirit." The person who devised the questionnaire had combed the gospels and epistles for "gifts" and discovered twenty-five categories of personal gifts that could be uncovered by matching certain descriptive statements to yourself.

Whenever I encountered a particular kind of statement, such as "I visit people who are in hospitals, jails, or nursing homes, and I feel blessed by it"; or, "It is important to me to be available to spend time with someone who needs a friend," I thought of my friend Louise. Louise was the one in my parish who made a casserole for new mothers or the newly bereaved, who always seemed available to drive an elderly parishioner to the doctor, who took the time to listen to the woman who needed to talk for hours on the telephone—and she did all those things as a matter of course. Louise made me feel guilty, because somehow I could not find time to do these things. The questionnaire freed me. Of course, Louise had the gift of "mercy"! I had discovered in answering the questionnaire that I had other gifts, such as "teaching," "faith," and, interestingly, "missionary," although I have not had occasion to explore that one.

We all have similar misconceptions about what "service to others" looks like. Louise's gift, being such an obvious example of service, intimidated me. But I have come to accept the fact that I am meant to use *my* gifts, not Louise's. Your gifts may not at first glance seem to have much to do with what you conceive of as "religion." But the fact of the matter is that, both in the church and the world around it, there is a need for what each of us has to offer.

For example, in the urban church with which I was once affiliated, with its large clergy and lay staff and a congregation marked by ethnic and economic diversity, there are some leaders who are visionaries, conceiving the future shape of the parish and its place in the community. There are people who take what those visionaries imagine and put the ideas into concrete form by structuring programs, writing proposals, or planning conferences. There are those on the staff who type the memoranda about the ideas, proofread them, and prepare them for mailing. There is the messenger who takes that mail to the mailroom. There are clergy who have a particular gift for preaching, and others who are gifted pastoral counselors. There are some, both lay and clergy, whose main focus is the liturgy. There is a music staff whose commitment is to produce the best that can be offered to God in worship, and a priest who oversees every detail of liturgical text and movement. There are the church school teachers, and the scholars who run a continuing education institute for clergy. There is the welcoming warmth of the woman who sits at the front desk in the parish office, and the courtesy of the vergers, who serve as the contact between the public and the parish. There are those whose gift is communication through the parish magazine and those whose gifts and training make a video program possible. There are those who run the bookstore with business acumen, those who are responsible for the parish's real estate investments, and those who deal with the business community regarding ethical issues. There are those who spend nights in the shelter for the homeless. There are those who prepare food in the parish dining room, and those who wash the dishes. There are those who keep the buildings clean, and those who keep them secure. I could go on and on.

While its resources and programs may be on a large scale, this church is not unlike the communities in which you live, in terms of the many possibilities for the use of your gifts. The important thing is to find what you most like to do, and to offer it. It is important also to remember that the whole world—not just "the church"—is your arena for the pastoral element of religion. What you do for the world need not *look* like religion, but religion it is, if you do it for the greater good of creation. You may decide to tutor children who need special attention, or to sit at a voter registration table. You may plant an organic garden, or encourage recycling in your community. You may write letters to those who are home-bound. You may raise a family. You may write books. Joseph Campbell's popular advice to "Follow your bliss" certainly applies to the pastoral endeavor; our contribution will most likely be fruitful in proportion to the zest we bring to it, and it is difficult to feel zest for something we do not like to do. Consider what the world would have lost if Thomas Aquinas had been convinced that holiness meant spending one's life on the streets of Paris ministering to the poor, or if Mother Teresa had felt she should devote her time to writing system-atic theology!

SPIRITUAL FRIENDSHIP
In addition to nurturing a rhythm of life, we can nurture our prayer through spiritual friendship. Because most people treat discussion of prayer with an almost Victorian discretion, you may have to exert some effort in this direction. It is a blessing to find a support group of kindred spirits or a spiritual friend with whom you can share your journey. Writer Edward J. Farrell noted:

Our Lord never sent anyone out alone. He always sent them in two's, two by two. We need to discover the law of the gospel and share our prayer with someone. In order to grow in prayer, one needs another person, someone to be brother or sister, something like a center for discernment, decision, fidelity. We have no lack of good will. Our greatest weakness is forgetfulness. We need to make our prayer more visible, our life more transparent. We need someone to help us to be faithful, to be obedient to our own inner grace.[3]

Our companion can be a theologian or a therapist, a spiritual director or simply a trusted friend. Such companionship can also come in part from spiritual reading. It was the autobiographies, letters, diaries, and poetry of the saints and mystics that introduced me to the world of prayer. Find the literary companions who are most congenial for you. They may be St. Augustine or Thomas Merton; St. Teresa of Avila or John Woolman; St. John of the Cross or Dag Hammarskjöld; Dante Alighieri or Evelyn Underhill; Henri Nouwen or Kathleen Norris; Martin Smith or Frederick Buechner. Companionship with these seekers will be a steady resource throughout your life.

THE BREATH OF LIFE

Sometimes our attention to God is very focused, in the foreground of our thoughts. Sometimes God is not in our conscious thoughts but is like the ground on which we stand and move—just there, although we do not notice it. The rhythm of conscious and unconscious awareness of God is a natural one, and each nourishes the other. Times of specific prayer focus help us live with recollection of God's presence, and our recollection in turn helps prepare us for those times when our attention is turned single-mindedly toward God. As with the rhythm of inhalation and exhalation, the ideal is balance. C. S. Lewis writes:

> It is well to have specifically holy places, and things, and days, for without these focal points or reminders, the belief that all is holy and "big with God" will soon dwindle into a mere sentiment. But if these holy places, things, and days cease to remind us, if they obliterate our awareness that all ground is holy and every bush (could we but perceive it) a Burning Bush, then the hallows begin to do harm. Hence both the necessity, and the perennial danger, of "religion."[4]

Just as specific times of physical exercise expand our breathing capacity so that our bodies can move through the day's activities with greater vigor, so our specific times of prayer "oxygenate" all of our life.

The underlying reality, in the words of St. Andrew of Crete, is that "while I breathe I pray." Prayer is our natural element, the breath of life. In the end, the source of all our prayer is not ourselves but the One who gave us life. Prayer is also our response to that One, through all the inhalations and exhalations of our life, from our first intake of air at the moment of birth to our final exhalation when, through the mysterious rhythm of death and resurrection, we enter a new and different life. Prayer is a discovery of who we are, and also of who we are called to become, as we open ourselves ever more fully to the breath of God that makes *adam* ever more human and more holy.

Breathing Space

Once again, find a relaxed position and pay attention to your breath. Notice the following about your breathing:

∾ What parts of my body move when I breathe?

∾ Is my breath fast, slow, or in between?

∾ What is the rhythm of my inhalations and exhalations?

> ☙ What is the texture of my breath? Even and smooth, or jerky and uneven?

> ☙ Is my breath deep or shallow?

> ☙ What adjectives might I use to describe the quality of my breath?

> ☙ What images might I use to describe my breathing?

Then consider the following questions:

> ☙ Have there been any changes in my breathing during the course of reading this book?

> ☙ Have there been any changes in my prayer during the course of reading this book?

> ☙ Am I more aware of my weight on the floor? What does this tell me about my identity as an "earthling"?

> ☙ Am I more aware of my breath as God's gift of life? What does this tell me about my identity as bearer of God's *ruach* in the world?

> ☙ In what ways am I called to breathe more fully, exploring all the varieties of prayer that bring me into closer relationship with God?

⤳ In what ways does God call me to stretch and move in the world around me?

Take some time to breathe quietly, allowing images and thoughts that this book has inspired rise like air bubbles from the water-creatures at the bottom of a deep pond. If one image or phrase especially strikes you, stay with it as you breathe, letting it become a window into the presence of God.

Conclude by standing, feeling both your rootedness in the earth through the soles of your feet and your spine stretching upward. Inhale, and reach your arms forward and upward above your head. Exhale, and open your arms outward toward the side, so that your body is in the shape of a cross.

Inhale and bring your hands inward toward the center of your chest at the level of your heart. Exhale and reach your hands forward and outward. You, bodyspirit, have just moved and breathed the prayer that concludes this book.

> In the name of our Creator,
> our Redeemer,
> and our Sustainer.
> *Amen.*

Endnotes

CHAPTER 1

LEARNING TO BREATHE AGAIN

1. Translation from the Episcopal *Book of Common Prayer,* hereafter BCP in the text.

CHAPTER 2

THE BREATH AND PREPARATION FOR PRAYER

1. For a more complete discussion of the subject, see Nancy Roth, *An Invitation to Christian Yoga* (Cambridge, Mass.: Cowley Publications, 2001).

CHAPTER 3

THE BREATH OF GOD AS SILENCE

1. Further suggestions for creating movement mantras are given in my *Invitation to Christian Yoga.*

2. Sylvia Shaw Judson, *The Quiet Eye: A Way of Looking at Pictures* (Chicago: Regnery Gateway, 1982), 1-2.

3. Frederick Franck, *The Awakened Eye* (New York: Random House, 1979), 47. See also Franck's *The Zen of Seeing* (New York: Random House, 1973).

4. T. S. Eliot, "The Dry Salvages," *Four Quartets,* from *The Complete Poems and Plays, 1909-1950* (New York: Harcourt, Brace and Company, 1952), 136.

5. Lawrence LeShan, *How to Meditate* (Boston: Little, Brown, 1974), 34, 32.

6. Joseph Campbell, *The Power of Myth* (New York: Doubleday, 1988), 13.

7. Brother Lawrence, *The Practice of the Presence of God* (London: A. R. Mowbray & Comapny), 29-30.

8. Douglas Steere, *On Being Present Where You Are* (Pendle Hill, Penn.: Pendle Hill, 1967), 35.

9. Kabir, quoted in Donna Farhi, *The Breathing Book: Good Health and Vitality Through Essential Breath Work* (New York: Henry Holt, 1996) 195.

CHAPTER 4
THE BREATH OF GOD AS THOUGHT

1. I have found Ann Faraday's *The Dream Game* (New York: Harper & Row, 1974) and Dream Power (New York: Berkley Publishing, 1972) and Morton Kelsey's *Dreams: A Way to Listen to God* (New York: Paulist Press, 1978) especially helpful.

CHAPTER 5
THE BREATH OF GOD AS SPEECH

1. These published collections of prayers from around the world include George Appleton, ed., *The Oxford Book of Prayer* (Oxford: Oxford University Press, 1985); Barbara Greene and Victor Gollancz, eds., *God of a Hundred Names* (London: Victor Gollancz, 1962); and *2000 Years of Prayer,* compiled by Michael Counsell (Harrisburg: Morehouse Publishing, 1999).

2. *A New Zealand Prayer Book: He Karakia Mihinare o Aotearoa* (Auckland, New Zealand: William Collins Publishers Ltd., 1989), 181.

CHAPTER 6
THE BREATH OF GOD AS ACTION

1. Dorothy Sayers, *Creed or Chaos* (New York: Harcourt Brace and Co., 1949), 46.

2. Lewis Thomas, *Lives of a Cell* (New York: Viking Press, 1974), 147-148.

CHAPTER 7
THE BREATH OF LIFE

1. Roy Menninger, "Responsibility to Self," in *Faithful Friendship*, Dorothy C. Devers, ed. (Cincinnati: Forward Movement Publications, 1980), 31.

2. Campbell, *Power of Myth*, 3.

3. Edward J. Farrell, "The Father is Very Fond of Me," in *Faithful Friendship*, 9.

4. C. S. Lewis, *Letters to Malcolm* (New York: Harcourt, Brace & World, 1964), 75.